SET TO STOCK MARKET

PRAKASH MAHAPATRA

To

My Readers & Clients

Contents

Preface *vii*

Acknowledgements *ix*

1. Introduction 1
2. Business & Its Form 3
3. Formation Of Companies 10
4. Shares & Debentures 16
5. Final Accounts Of Companies 23
6. Valuation & Anaysis Of Shares 28
7. Corporate Action 36
8. Ratio Analysis 40
9. Index & Market Index 45
10. Financial Market 48
11. Structure Of Financial Market 53
12. Mutual Fund 64
13. Commonly Used Terms In Stock Market 72
14. Recent Trend In Stock Market 78
15. Future & Option 84
16. Commodity Market 92
17. Foreign Market 97
18. Risk & Return 101
19. Tax Implication 108

Preface

The wide range of investment with innumerable complexities leads the investor confused, they often got confused by the various commission agent and misinterpretation in general. Today people got surplus fund to invest but due to lack of knowledge in avenue of investment they remain confused.

When answering question on investment, generally layman see themselves helpless and at the same time hopeless because where to invest? What amount to invest? How far it is secure? All these make them perplexed and disappointed.

All these above questions were in mind at the time of writing this book and I have tried upmost to present the same in a manner which would be easily understandable.

Acknowledgements

I am indebted to my teachers Shri K.C. Thakur Sir (Bhandaridah), Shri Srikant Das Sir (Rourkela) who has shaped my life. I have benefited from my seniors and friends at school as well as college.

I am grateful to my parents and family.

I am grateful to all at Notion Press for their contribution in bringing out book.

I look forward to receiving suggestions for improving the future editions of this work.

Prakash Mahapatra

prakash_bgr2003@yahoo.com

CHAPTER ONE

INTRODUCTION

After independence, socialism was given importance in India and hence there was no proper condition of investment. So to enhance investment, stock exchange facility was opened in few cities of India rather these were confined to metropolis cities. For this reason common men are not aware of stock markets.

In general, if we think of investment then the option available is Bank deposit, postal deposit and deposits in non-banking financial corporation. In India, there are many people who don't have idea about share market, even those got idea had negative idea, and most of them think it gambling. Even educated persons feel it gambling, the reason behind it are insufficient knowledge about share market. Such condition should not prevail. If we understand the technical terms used in the share market, what share is? How many types of shares are there? How transaction took place? How we can sell and purchase? How it is governed? What entity control it & etc. Then the myth of Gambling may vanish.

Now day's market so called share market is not confined to the metropolitan cities. It now crossed the boundaries of metropolitan cities and came down to the smaller town through satellite and computerized environment.

But going before share market one should understand the forms of business the legal entity of all those forms of business.

CHAPTER TWO

Business & Its Form

Business

Business includes trade, commerce and industries and is an economic activity. It includes any occupation in which people regularly engage in an activity with a view to earning profits. All those activities which are concerned with production and/or purchase and sale of goods and services with the purpose of selling them at a profit are business activity. The efforts and activities may be undertaken by individual, organization or enterprises which are engaged in industrial, commercial or professional activity. Activities are of two types viz. Economic and Non Economic activities, Economic actives are those which are carried out with motive to earn money like business, profession, job and etc. whereas Non Economic activities are those which are carried out without any motive to earn profit like marriage, puja, birthday, anniversary etc.

Trade - Includes the activities which are performed by retailer, wholesaler, stockiest, super stockiest and C&F agents. It is the process of taking goods from the source of production or place of procurement to the customer.

Commerce – otherwise known as aid or help to trade and includes transport, banking, warehousing, advertisement, insurance and etc. It includes all those activities which are necessary to bring goods and services from the place of origin to the place of consumption. It's a comprehensive term for all forms of trade, and all those services.

Industries – Industries are concerned with production of goods and services and it includes all those activities through which raw materials are converted into finished goods. Further industries can be categories into three viz. primary secondary and tertiary. Primary industry includes those activities concerned with extraction, production, processing of natural resources and reproduction of living species. Secondary industries are related to the processing of material which have been produced by primary industries. Tertiary or service industries deal with those activities, which helps the flow of goods and services from producer to ultimate customer.

FORMS OF BUSINESS

(I)Sole Proprietorship

(II)Partnership

(III)Company

(I) Sole Proprietorship

A person who started his business, mostly with his own resources or fund, and it need not required any legal formality. The owner and business are the same and the business liability may go even to his personal assets, business is generally on a small scale. A person one who setup the business with own resources. And bear alone the gains and risk of the business. Management and ownership lies in a single hand is one form of business.

Let think of a grocery shop, fancy store or a readymade garment shop, here we need say 2-3 lakhs of investment. Here one can invest and can take a risk to run the business. It is called a proprietary concern. Here in proprietary concern the investment and control over the business undertaken by one man or in the other words the management of business is the responsibility of a single man. The profit and loss arise by this particular business is confined and restricted to that individual.

(II) Partnership

The other form of business is partnership. Which is governed by "The Indian Partnership Act, 1932", under section 4 of The Indian Partnership Act, 1932 a partnership relation is "the relation between persons who have agreed to share the profits of a business carried on by all or any of them acting for all.

This definition brings forth the following three distinct elements, namely

i. Must be an agreement between the entire people concerned.
ii. The object of the agreement must be to share the profits and loss of a business.
iii. The business must be too carried on by all or any of them acting for all.

Persons who have entered into a partnership with one another are individually called as "PARTNERS" and collectively called as a "FIRM" and the name under which their business is carried on is called the "FIRM NAME". Here the investment and management may be by one or all partners.

Types of Partnerships

General Partnership

All the partners are collectively and personally liable for the liabilities of the Firm, it means that personal property of partners can be used to meet liabilities of the business. In India, most of the partnership are general partnership

Limited Partnership

The liability of at least one partner is limited, while liability of other partners may be limited. The person with limited liability called special partners while those with unlimited liability are called general partner. The liability of limited partner is limited to their capital in the business

Limited Liability Partnership

The liability of partners is limited to the unpaid amount of their shares, the private property of partners cannot be used to meet liabilities of the business, the change of partners does not affects the continuity of the partnership.

Partnership Deed

A document containing terms and condition of the partnership agreement is called partnership deed, the terms and condition rules regulations are put in writing on a stamp paper. It also contains duties and liabilities of partners.

Registration of Partnership

The registration of partnership is not compulsory under the Indian Partnership Act. However to avail certain advantages under law, the firm must be registered with Registrar of Firms of State.

A simple procedure is followed for getting a firm registered. The first thing to be done is to file an application with the Registrar of firms on a prescribed form. A registration fees is also deposited along with the application. The application should be signed and verified by each partner or any authorized agent. The particulars submitted to the Registrar are examined. It is also seen whether all legal formalities required, have been observed or not. If everything is in order, then the Registrar shall record an entry in the register of firms.

(III) Company

Another form of business is company. This is governed by "The Companies Act, 2013".Company is an association of those people who are running a business and have got themselves registered as a company. Those who purchase the shares of the company are called shareholders. Liability of every shareholder is limited. There is separate existence of the company and its shareholders. A company is organized by its directors under its common seal. Thus, a company is an artificial person recognized by law.

TYPE OF COMPANY

(A) According to Incorporation

(i) Chartered Companies – By Royal Charter Under this method a company is formed by Royal Charter of Company Law of England. East India Company is an example of this method.

(ii) Statutory Companies - Under a special Act of Parliament or state Legislature such companies are formed, generally companies for public utility services are formed under special statutes. These companies are given wide power and may or may not use "Limited". Examples of such companies are Reserve Bank of India, State Trading Corporation of India and etc.

(iii) Registered Companies - These are companies formed and registered under the provision of the Companies Act. Most of the companies in India are registered under the Indian Companies Act.

(B) **According to Liability**

(i) Company Limited By Share –It is that company whose capital is divided into shares and liability of each shareholder is limited to the extent of the amount of shares hold by him.

(ii) Company Limited By Guarantee – There is such companies where the liability of each shareholder is limited to the amount of guarantee which he undertakes to fulfill at the time of liquidation of the company. Such companies are not formed with the intention of earning a profit. Chamber of commerce, charitable institution clubs, and societies are example of such companies.

(iii) Unlimited Company- In these companies liability of each member is unlimited. Practically such companies are not formed.

(C) According to ownership

(i) Government Companies – A government company is that in which at least 51% of the capital has been subscribed by state or central government or jointly by state and central government. Central govt. is empowered to make necessary changes in the companies act in order to manage and organize the govt. company. Govt. companies are audited in consultations with Comptroller and Auditor General. The annual report of every government company is presented before the parliament.

(ii) Holding & subsidiaries Companies – If a company control the polices of another company through the ownership of its share, i.e. if it holds more than 51% shares of another company , the company is called Holding company. A company the policies of which are controlled is called a subsidiaries company. A holding and a subsidiary company are separate companies having separate legal identity.

(D) **According to Transferability of share**

(i) Public Company - The companies Act defines a public company as one which is not a private company and registered under the Act. The member of a public company can be maximum to the limit of its capital. There is no restriction on sale or transfer of its shares and the company can invite the public to purchase its share.

(ii) Private Company - A private company is said to be a private limited company which is subject to three restrictions viz.

(a) It cannot issue its share to the public

(b) The number of shareholders must not exceed to specified number.

(c) It cannot allow open transfer of shares to the public.

(E) According to Nationality

(i) Indian Company – A company incorporated in India as per the companies Act whether operating in India or outside India is called Indian company

(ii) Foreign Company – A company incorporated outside India but has a place of business in India is called Foreign company.

(F)According to Public Interest

(i) Small Company – A small company means a company other than public company.

a. Paid up capital of which does not exceed fifty lakhs or
b. Turnover of which as per last profit & loss account does not exceed two crores Rupees

(ii) One Person Company – A one person company is a one shareholder corporate entity, where legal and financial liability is limited to the company.

CHAPTER THREE

Formation of Companies

Formation of companies in India is done by promoters. In Our country history of promoters starts with the history of companies. A promoter is a person who forms a company and gives it a practical shape. In India, the work of promotion has been done by the managing agents.

There is the need of a man who will discover the opportunities to make money, investigate such proposition, assemble and finance them, and there by produce a going concern. The man who performs these functions is known as a promoter. A promoter may be an individual firm or even a company.

PREPARTION AND FILLING OF DOCUMENT

(I) MEMORANDUM OF ASSOCIATION

The first and foremost important work of the promoter is to prepare the memorandum of association of the company. It has been described as the charter of the company. Because it lays down in precise and clear terms the objectives of the company, defines the scopes of its operation and its relation with the investor and outside the world. The company has to work within the limits laid down in the memorandum .MOA is printed, drafted into paragraphs consecutively numbered. It has to be signed by at least seven persons in case of public limited company and atleast two person in case of private limited company with their full address in presence of one witness.

It is the principal document of the company and no company can be registered without memorandum of association. The purpose of memorandum is to explain the scope of activities.

Clauses of memorandum

1. Name Clause – Being a separate entity it must have name, the name should not be objectionable in the opinion of Government. The word "Limited" must be added at the end of the name. A company may select a name which does not resemble the name of any other company, there are certain more provisions relating to name clause which are strictly prohibited details must be checked before considering name

2. Registered Office Clause – Company should have a registered office, the place of office must be intimated to the Registrar within 30 days of incorporation or commencement of business whichever is earlier. A company can shift its registered office after considering the provisions lay down.

3. Object Clause – No activity can be taken by the company which is not mentioned in the object clause. It determines the rights and power of the company and also the sphere of activities.

4. Liability Clause – This clause state the liability of the member is limited to the value of share held by them, members are liable to only the unpaid balance of their shares. The liability of share may be limited by guarantee.

5. Capital Clause – This clause state the total capital of the proposed company. The division of capital into equity

shares and preference share capital should be mentioned, the number of shares in each category and their value should be given.

6. Association clause – The memorandum must be signed by at least seven person in case of public company and by at least two person in case of private limited company. This clause contains the names of signatories to the memorandum of association. Each subscriber must take at least one share in the company. The subscriber declare that they agree to incorporate the company and agree to take the shares stated against their name.

7. Name of Nominee in case of One Person Company – In case of one person company, memorandum must state the name of the person who, in the event of the death of the subscriber or his inability to act shall become the member of the company.

(II) ARTICLE OF ASSOCIATION

The article of association is a document containing the rules and regulation for the internal management of the company. It is called By law of the company. AOA are prepared on the basis of MOA. AOA should be printed and divided into paragraph and be signed by each subscribers to the memorandum, in presence of at least one witness. The article embodies the powers of the directors and officers and of the shareholders as to voting etc. The mode and form in which changes in the internal regulation of the company may from time to time be made.

The rule and regulations which are framed for the internal management of the company are set out in a document named article of association. It is a supplementary document to the memorandum of association. The private company limited by share, companies limited by guarantee and unlimited company must have their article of association. A company limited by share may or may not frame its own article of association, such company may adopt all or any of the regulation contained in the model set of Articles given in **Table A in Schedule I** of the act.

Contents of Article of Association

(i) Share capital and their value and their division into equity and preference shares

(ii) Rights of each class of share

(iii) Procedure relating to the allotment of share

(iv) Rules relating to transfer of transmission of shares

(v) Appointments, remuneration, power, duties of the directors and officer of the company

(vi) Procedure for conversion of shares into stock into share and vice versa

(vii) Notice of meeting, voting rights of member, proxy, quorum, poll etc.

(viii) Audit of Accounts, transfer of amount of reserves, declaration of dividend.

(ix) Borrowing power of the company.

(x) Winding up of the company. And etc.

The article of association can be altered by passing special resolution. However certain restrictions are imposed on the nature and extent of the alteration that may be made.

(a) The change should not violate the provisions of the company's law.

(b) It should not be contrary to the provisions of memorandum of association.

(c) The alteration must not have anything illegal.

(d) The alteration should not affect the minority interest.

(III) PROSPECTUS

A public company has to prepare its prospectus or a statement in lieu of prospectus before it can start its business. A prospectus is issued to invite the public to purchase its shares or debentures. A copy of the prospectus has to be sent to the office of the Registrar. Any notice, circular, advertisement or any other invitation offering to the public for subscription or purchase of any shares and debenture of a company would be considered as a prospectus whether it's called as such or not. It is a valuable document supporting the structure of the company.

A prospectus is a document, notice, circular, advertisement issued for inviting public to subscribe to the shares of the company.

Prospectus should have the following essentials

(i) There must be an invitation to offering to the public.

(ii) The invitation must be made on behalf of the company.

(iii) The invitation must be to subscribe or purchase.

(iv) The invitation must relate to share or debenture.

CERTIFICATE OF INCORPORATION

When all the required documents are filed with Registrar along with the requisite fees, a scrutiny is made. If all the documents are found in order, the Registrar will enter the name of the company in the register of the companies and issue a certificate of Incorporation. The date mentioned in the certificate is the date of incorporation of the company. A private limited company can start its business with this certificate, but a public limited company can start business only after Business commencement certificate.

CERTIFICATE OF THE COMMENCEMENT OF BUSINESS

A public company has to obtain the certificate of commencement of business before starting its business. Thus following additional documents have to be filed with the registrar.

a. Prospectus or a statement in lieu of prospectus.
b. Preparing allotment return after the allotment of shares
c. A declaration by the officers of the company that legal formalities have been completed.

CHAPTER FOUR

Shares & Debentures

A share is the interest of shareholders in the company measured by a sum of money for the purpose of liability and of interest (dividend). It also consists of other rights given by articles. Authorized capital of a company is split up into units with definite face value, called shares. In other words we can say "the large capital of a company is divided in equal parts and each part is known as share". Mainly three types of shares are there.

a. Preference share
b. Equity or Ordinary share
c. Deferred shares or founder share

(a) Preference share – A preference share is given the right of priority in respect of payment of dividend and in respect of return of capital, in case the company being wound up. And are subject to certain limitation, in regards to voting rights. These are entitled to have the fixed rate of dividend out of the net profit of the company. These shares considered safe investment, permanent income and less risk. However preference shares are further categories in various ways like cumulative preference shares, non-cumulative preference shares, redeemable preference share non- redeemable preference share, participating preference share, non-participating preference share, convertible preference share, non-convertible preference shares and etc.

TYPES OF PREFERNCE SHARE

i. Convertible Preference Shares – The holders of this share may be given a right to convert their holdings into equity shares after specific period.
ii. Non Convertible Preference Share – The share which cannot be converted to equity share are non convertible preference share.
iii. Cumulative Preference Share – These shares have the right to claim dividend for those years also where there are no profits. In such shares dividend goes on cumulating unless otherwise it is paid.
iv. Non Cumulative Preference Share – The holders of such share have no claims for the arrears of dividend.
v. Redeemable Preference Share – Neither the company can return the share capital nor the share holders can demand for repayment, if redeemable preference shares are issued the company has the right to redeem.
vi. Non Redeemable Preference Share – Those share which cannot be redeemed unless company liquidate or winding up.
vii. Participating Preference Share – If some profits remain after paying dividend to both the class of shareholders then such preference shareholders participates in the surplus profits.
viii. Non Participating Preference Shares – The shares on which only a fixed rate of dividend is paid are known as

non participating preference shares.

(b) Ordinary share or Equity share – Those shares which are not preference share are equity shares. They are paid dividend out of the net profit of the company after the preference shareholders have been paid fixed rate of dividends. Equity shares are those shares which carry no special rights in respect of annual dividends and return of capital after the company is wound up. If in any particular year, there are no profits or insufficient profits, they are not entitled to receive anything. On the other hand, if company earns more profit, they get a higher rate of dividend. They have the extensive rights in the management of the company.

(c)Deferred share or Founder shares – No public company can issue deferred shares. It are those shares which participate in the profit of the company only after the claims of all other shareholders have been met. These shares were ordinarily issued to promoters or founder of the company prior to 1956. These were of Re 1/- each having one share one vote. Thus directors used to retain these shares with them. They had special rights to vote in company's meetings.

Stock

When a company has received the full paid value of its shares, it can convert the amount received into its stocks. Which can further divided into smaller parts of any amount."Each part of share is stock".

Dividend

Distribution of divisible or distributable profits of a company among the holders of its shares. Dividend is paid by a company to its shareholder on the basis of number of shares held by them and the rights attaching to the various classes of shares. The question of payment of dividend does not arise in the absence of profit. Quantum of dividend depends on a number of factors.

- Profit earned by a company.
- Terms of issue of various classes of shares.
- Dividend policy of the company.
- Legal restriction on payment of dividend and etc.

Preference shareholders enjoy a preferential right over the equity shareholders in the matter of dividend. They are entitled to receive dividend at the fixed rate before any dividend is paid to equity shareholders.

Interim dividend

Interim dividend means a dividend paid to the shareholders of a company in anticipation of profits of a period before the accounts of the company for that period have been prepared.

Bonus Share

When a company accumulates huge reserve out of its profit which is much in excess of the needs of the company, the excess amount can be distributed by way of bonus share among the existing shareholder of a company. By issue of bonus shares there is reduction in the amount of accumulated profits & reserve and a corresponding increase in the paid- up share capital of the company. Hence the accumulated profits & reserve of the company are converted into its share capital which is permanently used in the business.

Right Share

A company is under legal obligation to offer first the further issue of shares to its existing equity shareholder. But the holders are not liable to necessarily accept the offer so made. They have the option of rejection or renunciation. This right is called right issue. There is specific advantage of this legal right to the existing shareholder specially when the market price of the share is more than the issue price. The moment a right issue is made, the quotation of the existing shares tend to go up.

Debenture

A company cannot issue shares more than its authorized capital. If the need arises it can raise loan from public. This type of borrowing is affected by issue of debentures. A debenture is a written acknowledgement of debt by the company under its common seal usually secured by a charge on company's assets containing provision for the payment of interest and an undertaking to repay the debt at a specific date or at intervals or at the option of the company. As per the companies Act debenture "includes stock, bond or any other securities of a company whether consisting a charge on the assets of the company or not". Thus debenture is the record of indebtness accompany for its exposure and development may use this source of finance to raise funds without increasing its share capital. Debentures are of different type in view of repayment, negotiability or transferability, security and conversion.

Thus company may invite the public by open declaration to lend money, for a fixed period at a declared rate to be paid on such money. Debenture is an instrument in writing given by a company acknowledging the liability for the total amount received as a result of issue of debentures and agreeing thereby to pay the money so raised after the expiry of the stipulated period at a certain rate of interest per annum.

TYPES OF DEBENTURE

A. Registered Debenture – Person on whose names appear in the register of debenture are liable to get back the principal amount maturity.
B. Bearer Debenture – Those debenture which can be transfer by way of delivery and company does not have record, the interest on bearer debentures is paid by mean of attached coupons. On maturity the principal amount is paid to the bearer.
C. Irredeemable Debenture – A debenture which contains no clause of payment, but since it is a loan and repayable only on winding up or liquidation.
D. Redeemable Debenture – On the expiry of specific time the company return back the debenture holders the principal amount.
E. Debenture Issued as Collateral – Debenture issued as collateral security means, in case the loan is repaid the debenture issued as collateral security are automatically redeemed. The lender can realize the collateral security in case borrower fails to make the payment.
F. Naked Debenture – when debentures are issued without any charge or mortage such debenture are Naked debenture.
G. Secured Debenture – When any property is offered as security or collateral such debenture are secured debenture.
H. Convertible Debenture – Those Debenture where option is given to convert them into equity or preference share at stated rates of exchange, after a time period.

Bond

A bond is a debt instrument where rate of interest is not predetermined. A bond is promise to pay by the issuer of the Bond the principal with interest at a particular date of maturity to the investor.

TYPES OF BOND

A. Zero Coupon Bond – Such bonds are sold at discount from the face value and have zero interest rate. The difference between the face value and cost of acquisition is the gain to the investor.
B. Deep Discount Bond – A bond that is sold at significantly lesser value than its par value, risk is eliminated in such type of bond. Difference between the sale price and original cost of acquisition will be treated as capital gain.
C. Junk Bond – Junk bonds are corporate bond with low rating.

CHAPTER FIVE

Final Accounts of Companies

A company is under legal obligation to keep proper books of accounts and to prepare its final account every year in the prescribed manner. Final Accounts of a company consist of the following two statements.

a. Balance sheet as at the end of the accounting period disclosing the financial position of the company.
b. Profit and loss Account for that period disclosing the result of the operations of the company.

While preparing every company must conform to certain legal requirement as contained in the companies Act. After the final accounts of a company are prepared the same must be audited by qualified auditors, i.e. person who are practicing chartered accountant. It is desirable to make out the Profit & Loss A/c namely.

a. Trading Accounts
b. Profit and Loss Accounts
c. Profit and Loss Appropriation Accounts

To know separately the gross profit or loss, the net profit or loss and the disposition of the net profit if any.

However, during the course of audit, several doubts and queries may be raised by the auditors. Doubt and queries generally relate to those points where the auditors feel that standard practices have not been followed. Auditors go on making notes of all such doubts and after the audit is completed the points of difference are discussed with the management. If the auditors feel satisfied with the explanations offered, they drop the audit query and if they are not satisfied with the explanations they include such difference notes on accounts or in the audit report. The Board of Directors generally offers their comments on those points of difference as clarifications for the consumption of the public and the shareholders.

BASICS OF PROFIT AND LOSS ACCOUNTS (P&L)

Statement of Profit and loss which is prepared by company in order to know the profit earned and the loss sustained during a specified period. It contains information on the revenue, cost and profitability during that specified period. Final audited P&L statements are published with the annual report.

Items Posted in Profit and Loss Account.

a. Net Sales – Both cash and credit sales are included, sales return should be deducted and net amount is shown as gross sale, however applicable GST has to be deducted from the gross sale to arrive net sales.
b. Direct Expenses – These include all expenses which have been incurred before the goods ready for sale. Examples of these type of expenses may be cost of raw material, carriage inward, wages and salary, motive power, coal, gas, fuel and etc. Lower the direct cost

higher operating efficiency. Cost can be categorize further in terms of variable and fixed cost. The cost structure exposes risks when business slows down.

c. EBITDA – Earning before Interest and Tax Depreciation and Amortization is the difference between Net sales and Direct Costs. Higher the EBITDA better the company.
d. Depreciation/Amortization - It is an expenses due to wear and tear, la pse of time and exhaustion of asset used in the business, the loss sustained by fixed assets are depreciation amortization is the term used for depreciation of intangible assets like copyright, patent and etc. Depreciation / Amortization are shown as expenses but there is no actual cash outflow. Deducting Depreciation / Amortization from EBITDA gives us EBIT.
e. Interest – Interest paid on loans, overdrafts, interest paid to debenture holders, bond and bills overdue is an expenses and is deductible from EBIT, whereas if interest received on loans advance by the company, on deposits and on securities is a gain and added to EBIT.
f. PBT – Deducting Depreciation / Amortization and interest from EBITDA and then adding interest or other gains to give us the total profit of the company for the period after meeting all the expenses. Tax need to be paid on this profit is known as Profit before Tax.
g. Tax – This amount is deducted from PBT, as the rate prescribed by Government from time to time.
h. PAT – This is the final amount which remains with the company after paying all obligation to the stakeholders other than the shareholders. This amount may be paid out as dividend or may be retained in the company partially or fully for further growth or expansion.

Items in Balance Sheet

A Balance sheet is a statement prepared with a view to measure the financial position of a company on a certain fixed date. The financial position of a company is indicated by its Assets (application of funds) on the given date and its liabilities (sources of funds) on that date. It is a statement and not an account. A properly drawn up balance sheet gives information relating to the nature and value of assets, the nature and extent of liabilities, whether the company is solvent, whether the company is overtrading. Assets (application of funds) and liabilities (source of funds) must match at aggregate level, both the side of balance sheet must match at all the time.

i. Share Capital – Share capital means capital raised by the company by issue and subscription of shares. Shareholders are the persons to whom shares are allotted and they are the owner's of the company to the extent of their shareholding. It include both Preference and equity shares.

j. Reserve and Surplus – It denotes the amounts set aside or held back out of profits to meet any future requirement or contingency. The purpose behind reserve creation of reserves is to safeguard the financial position against any unforeseen losses or liabilities. Thus this is shareholders money, while share capital is contributed capital, reserve and surplus is retained capital. Apart from the reserve created out of retained profits, balance sheet shows other reserve which are made out of capital profit like capital reserve, share premium and reserve capital.

k. Networth – Share capital and reserve & surplus together represent the shareholder's fund or Networth or owner's capital.

ax. Long Term Debt – Any debt taken for a period more than 12 months from the date of balance sheet or after the operating cycle. This may be in the form of loans taken by financial institution or debt securities issued as debenture or bond. Investor prefer companies with low debt.

all. Current Liabilities – Those debts or obligations that are due, must be settled within a period of 12 months, current liabilities are analysis to determine the efficiency with which working capital are managed.

Profit and Loss Accounts and balance Sheet do not focus on cash flow since accounting is on accrual basis. Due to this there is difference between profits and the actual cash with the business. Hence one more statement are prepared i.e." Cash Flow Statement ".

Cash Flow Statement provide information about the passage of cash in and out of an organization during a stipulated time frame.

CHAPTER SIX

Valuation & Anaysis of Shares

Normally the price prevailing on the stock exchange is accepted. However valuation by experts is called for when parties involved in the transaction/deal/scheme etc. fail to arrive at mutually accepted value.

Whenever a buying price and a selling price coincide, a sale occurs. Roughly classification of buyers may be made as

- Informed and analytical investor
- Informed speculator
- The uninformed

Similarly a rough classification of seller is

- Informed and analytical seller
- Informed speculator
- The uninformed
- Those with an urgent need to sell

In a stock exchange numerous people collect some to deal some to watch and some to rig and consequently depending on the motivation they react and the results of such reaction came out as market price. Thus stock exchange price is a price pure and simple and not a value based on valuation. Stock exchange price is basically determined on the interaction of demand and supply and business cycle. Valuation of share should be meaning full. Valuation of shares may be broadly classified as under.

- Asset-Backing or intrinsic value method.
- Yield Basis method.
- Fair Value method.

ASSET BACKING METHOD OR INTRINSIC VALUE METHOD

Since the valuation is made on the basis of the assets of the company, it is known as asset basis or asset backing method. Under this method value of the net asset of the company is to be determined first. Thereafter the net assets are to be divided by the number of shares in order to find out the value of each share, value of goodwill and investment are added with net assets, if there are any preference shares, those are deducted with their arrear dividend from the net assets. Thus practically we can present this valuation method as under

A. Computation of Total Assets

Total Assets =

Fixed Assets + Current Assets + Investment (market Value) + Goodwill (if any)

A. Computation of Total Liabilities

Total Liabilities =

Long Term Liabilities + Current Liabilities + Debenture + Preference Share Capital +Arrears of Dividend (if any)

Net fund available for equity share holders will be A – B

i.e. Total assets minus Total liabilities.

Intrinsic value = (Fund available for equity shareholder)/ (No of equity share)

YIELD BASIS METHOD

The effective rate of return on investment which is invested by the investor. Since the valuation of share is made on basis of yield, it is called yield basis method. Under this method valuation is made on the basis of

- Profit
- Dividend

Profit

Here profit ascertained on the basis of past average profit. Then capitalized value of profit is to be determined on the basis of normal rate of return and capitalized value of profit is divided by the number of shares in order to find the value of each share.

Capitalized value of share = (Profit) / (Normal Rate of Return) x 100

Value of each equity share = (Capitalized Value of Each Share) / (No. Of Shares)

Dividend

Valuation of share may be made either on the basis of total amount of dividend or on the basis percentage or rate of dividend. The shareholding minimum number of shares (minority holding) may determine the value of shares on dividend basis, since he has to satisfy himself having the rate of dividend, as he has no power to control the affairs, on the other hand, the shareholders (majority holding) has got much controlling rights over the affairs of the company including the recommendation for the rate of dividend among others.

Value of each equity share =

(Rate of Dividend) / (Normal Rate Of Return) x Paid Up Value Of Equity

Fair value method

Most expert do not prefer to use intrinsic value or yield value, they prefer fair value method, which is the mean of intrinsic value and yield value method.

Fair Value = (Intrinsic value + yield value) / 2

Share / Stock Analysis

Analysis is to understand and evaluate the growth of the companies and Industries. Share / stock analysis helps in formulating investment and trading techniques. Stock Analysis deals with the performance of the stock in particular and the Index in general. There are many factors that affecting the collecting moods at the stock market. Stock market is dynamic it keeps changing with every information. It is presumed that every investor to be rational who invest by considering all the information available to them like company specific news, monetary and fiscal policy, economic and political conditions, international stock market and etc. While analyzing companies and industries, one must focus on changes on macro economic factors like monetary and fiscal policy and their impact on the economy, flow from FDI (foreign Direct Investment) and other global factors that impact GDP (Gross Domestic Product). Macro economics analysis show the impact on different industries and then to search a business in the industry, but some news or information on same company, which may move to industry analysis to see whether industry and economy favors the company. Companies must be analyzed in qualitative and quantitative dimensions, qualitative is non mathematical where as quantitative is mathematical in nature. Stock analysis is basically of two types.

(A) Fundamental Analysis.

(B) Technical Analysis.

(A) Fundamental Analysis

Fundamental analysis consists of both qualitative and quantitative factors. By considering the macro economics factor that could have an effect on the value of the stock analysis are made. It may include financial, economic, or industry specific factors, management efficiency, competitive position among its industry rivals. Along with this fundamental analysis rely on the facts of Balance Sheet for arriving book value with some specific factors like sales figure, earning of the company, Assets and Liabilities of the companies are analyzed. Fundamental Analysis studies the strength of the company which is effective in long run of the stock price rather than in short run. Fundamental analysis checks.

Balance Sheet – Here Assets and Liabilities are recorded. It is always desirable for company to have Assets are greater than the Liabilities, it reflects sound financial conditions.

Return on Assets – It measures the profitability of a company, how much it has earned by deploying Assets. This shows the company's strength.

Net Income – For any business Net Income is bottom line which needs to analyze before investment.

Revenue – Inflow of cash indicates the demand scenario of company's product which may indicates it growth.

Fundamental analysis is a part of stock market analysis which uses the fundamental aspect of the companies and the economy as a whole for predicting the upcoming price of the particular stock.

The price prevailing in market is called market price (MP) and the price justified by the fundamentals is called fair value (FV). If the market price of a security is higher than the fair value which is justified by fundamental factors, sell that security. Sooner or later market realizes the mistake and the price of stock may go down. However to sell this particular stock be based on its fundamentals, it must be before the market correct its mistake from the increased price. If the market value is less than the fair value justified by the fundamental factors, buy that stock. And if the market price and face value are equal, then no action.

Stock valuation depends on future earning and the estimates of growth in earnings. But Efficient Market Hypothesis contradicts this concept of prediction. EMH propagates stock price incorporate and reflect all relevant information. It gain propagate a market in which information is quickly reflected accurately in share prices, it means that current level is on unbiased estimate at its true economic value based on the information revealed.

(B) Technical Analysis

Technical analysis is based on assumption, all information can affect the performance of a stock, economic and industry factor, market sentiments are reflected in its stock price. Technical analysis is not concerned with fundamental of the business. Instead, Technical analysis approaches to forecast the direction of the price by study of historical pattern considering price and volume. Such analysis assumes that historical price gives indication about its future performance, it use chart and other statistical tools to identify the pattern of stock. Technical analysis considers price movements are repetitive in nature. While analyzing technical, long and short term market trend volume of trade, moving average, candle stick, relative strength index etc. are considered which may indicate the future movement of stock.

Market activity generates indicators price trends that can be used to forecast the direction and magnitude of stock price movement. To understand price behavior one need to analyze the historical prices which provides indicators of the underlying trends and its direction along with this it need to understand the volume that accompanies price movement, which provides inputs on the underlying strength of the trend. And the time span over which price and volumes are observed that influence price over a period of time.

Integrating all these into price charts, points of support and resistance in chart and price trends are traced, support and resistance levels represents a point there is lot of buying and selling interest and the implication on the price if support and resistance level is broken.

Few Techniques in Technical Analysis

Fibonacci /number

Leonardo Fibonacci (1170 – 1240) was a medieval mathematician who discover the series of numbers, 1, 1, 2, 5, 8, 13, 21, ... After the initial pair of ones, each succeeding number is simply the sum of the previous number. Technical Analyst follow Fibonacci numbers usually make use of the number 1.618. The number is called golden mean. After the first ten numbers in the series, each Fibonacci number divided by its immediate predecessor equals 1.618.

The investment business uses the first two ratio 0.382 and 0.618 to compare to compute retracement levels of a previous move. Some analyst keep close tab on resistance and support level as predicated by the Fibonacci ratios. When the stock price approaches important Fibonacci level, unusual things can occur.

Eliott Wave Principle

R.N.Eliott (1871 -1948) develops this principle and being used by various market participants. It suggest that stock price move in clear trend and stock prices move between optimism and pessimism of all market participants psychology and wide swings in the participants psychology makes stock prices move in certain pattern / trend.

Dow Theory

C.H. Dow (1851 – 1902) considered as the father of Technical Analysis, however he neither wrote nor published his complete theory on market but his associates have published his work. The Dow Theory is made up of six basic principles.

1. The stock market discounts all information
2. Stock market has three trends viz. primary trend, secondary trend and minor trend.
3. Primary trend has three phases viz. accumulation phase, participation phase and distribution phase
4. Stock market Indexes must confirm each other.
5. Volume must confirm the trend.
6. Trend remains intact until and unless clear reversal.

Thus Fundamental Analysis involves macroeconomic, industry analysis and company analysis where as Technical Analysis focuses at the trade volume and the movement of the price along with it concentrates on the change of the price.

CHAPTER SEVEN

Corporate Action

Corporate action is an event that brings a change to the securities either equity or debt already issued by the company and ultimately it put impact the shareholders value and financial structure of the company. As a result there is an impact on share price. However such actions are taken with the motive to increase profitability and shareholders benefits. During such corporate action, the company announce a record date and book closure period and investors whose name appears on the records on this date become eligible to receive notice of the actions and benefits. All corporate action in India need to follow the requirements prescribed by certain regulation laid below.

Provisions of the Companies Act.

Relevant regulations of SEBI.

Terms of listing agreement entered into with the stock exchange

(I)Stock Split

Where the face value of the existing shares is reduced in a defined ratio and as a result the numbers of share increases and it boost the stock liquidity despite of this action markets cap remain the same. In shareholders perspective proportionate ownership remains unchanged and number of shares held by them go up, at overall ownership level, there is no negative impact to the shareholders. For example a stock split of 1:10 means split of an existing share into 5 shares. Accordingly face value of shares will go down to $1/10^{th}$ of the original face value. If an investor hold 100 shares of a company with face value Rs.10/- each, a stock split in the ratio 1:5 will increase the number of shares held by him to 1,000 and the face value will fo down to Rs. 1/-.

(II) Share Consolidation

Consolidation of share is reverse of stock split, here company changes the structure of its share capital by increasing the par value of its share in a defined ratio and reduce the number of shares. If the prices of the shares in the secondary market are seen to be low effecting the perception of investor, consolidations are made. An increase in the price per share after consolidation, leads to better perception among the market participants. For example, if an investor hold 1,000 shares of a company with face value Rs.1/- , a stock consolidation in the ratio 10:1 will reduce the number of shares to 100 but the face value of the share will go up to Rs.10/-. From company perspective there is no change in its share capital since decrease in the number of shares is offset by corresponding increase in the face value. Shareholders proportionate ownership remains unchanged and number of share go down.

(III) Merger & Acquisition

A merger is a combination of two companies into one large company. An acquisition is the buying of one company by another. Acquisition usually refers to a purchase of smaller company by a large one, when a smaller company acquires larger established company it is called" Reverse Merger". Merger and other types of acquisition are performed in the hopes of realizing economic gain. Some of the advantages of merger and acquisitions include economies of scale, combining complementary resources, tax advantage and eliminating inefficiencies. The shareholding pattern of a listed company may change due to a substantial of shares and voting rights by an acquirer and person acting in concert with the acquirer. SEBI (Substantial acquisition of shares and takeover) 1997, provide relevant triggers and requirements for an acquirer and offer an opportunity to public shareholders to exit from the company in such a situation they choose.

(IV) Buy Back of Shares

Stock which is bought back by the issuing company, reducing the amount of outstanding stock in on the open market. Companies do this when they feel that their stock is undervalued on the open market. Other time, for stock repurchase is to protect the company from takeover threat, motive of buy back of shares could be multiple. Apart from the motive, buy back of share can be done only out of reserve & surplus available with the company. Share buyback leads to a reduction in its share capital, even if there is no change in Profit & loss. Due to buyback it would result in increased EPS and shareholders may enjoy higher dividend. Ultimately market value per share goes up.

(V) Loan Restructuring

It is a method used by the company who are unable to meet their obligation towards debt. The process of debt restructuring involves analyzing debt position, meeting with the lenders and providing them information regarding current and future financial position. For restructuring the debt by modification, this may include the amount of loan, rate of interest, mode of repayment, funds and/or equity of the company. A restructuring exercise is the advantage of the borrower and lender.

(VI) Share swap

Exchange of something is swap, hence share swap means exchanging one set of shares with another set of share. Share swapping occurred when there is merger and acquisition. Before the swap occurs each party must accurately value its company. Before the swap ratio is calculated.

(VII) Delisting of Share

It refers to permanent removal of the company shares from being listed in stock exchange. Delisting may be compulsory or voluntary. Any delisting either compulsory or voluntary has to happened as defined in the regulation by SEBI

(VIII) Bonus Issue

Bonus shares are issued to the existing shareholders by the company without any consideration, it is an alternative to cash dividend. The shareholders do not pay anything for these shares, there is no change in the value of their holding either in pre bonus or post bonus stages. The company makes the bonus issue out of its free reserve. Bonus issuance is known as capitalization of reserve.

(IX) Right Issue

Company which wants to raise more capital through an issue of share must offer to the existing share holders and such offers of shares is called Right share. Share under right issues are generally offered at a discount to the prevailing market price. As a result of right issue, total number of shares goes up with a corresponding amount increase in the cash of the balance sheet.

CHAPTER EIGHT

Ratio Analysis

A ratio is a number expressed in terms of another number and calculated by dividing one item or figure with the other. It shows the quantitative relationship that exists between two figures or item. Accounting ratio is used to show the relationship which exists in the published accounts and financial statement and is employed for comprising the working result and determining the efficiency of the capital by comprising its capital assets liabilities and sales with that of other concerns engaged in the same industry.

Ratio analysis are not only useful for internal management, it is equally useful for the prospective investor, creditors and outsiders. Ratios are the best instrument for testing solvency liquidity, profitability and management efficiency of any business. Ratio may be broadly classified as follows.

a. Balance sheet ratio

---- Current ratio
---- Working capital ratio
---- Liquidity ratio

a. Revenue statement ratio

---- Gross profit ratio
---- Operating profit ratio
---- Expenses ratio
---- Net profit ratio

c. Balance sheet and revenue statement ratio

---- Turnover ratio
---- Net profit to total asset ratio
---- Proprietary ratio
---- Return on proprietors fund ratio

There are many other ratios some of those which are useful to us in context of stock are elaborated briefly.

Return on shareholder or proprietors fund

= (Net Profit after tax) / (Proprietors or Shareholder funds)

This ratio indicates how profitably proprietors fund being used and is considered a very effective measure to test the overall profitability of the business. Higher the ratio greater the financial strength and better is the return.

Return on shareholder equity

= (Net profit after Tax) / (Shareholder Equity)

This is the ratio of net profit to equity shareholders. High ratio stands for better security of dividend payment to the equity shareholder and greater financial strength of the business.

Return on capital employed

= (Net profit after Tax) / (Capital Employed)

It indicates how efficiently capital employed has been used in the business. Higher the ratio, better the management efficiency and greater is the profitability of the business, Low ratio is the sign of over capitalization and poor management efficiency in the use of capital employed.

Dividend coverage ratio

= (Net profit after tax & Preference dividend) /(Equity Dividend)

It indicates the relationship between available net profit after tax and preference dividend and equity dividend. It shows the number of times equity dividend is covered by the available profit. Higher the coverage, greater is the financial strength and fair is the return to the shareholders.

Dividend yield ratio

= (Dividend per Share paid) / (Market price per Share)

It indicates rate of dividend received by the shareholder not on the face value of shares but on the market price of the shares. This ratio is useful to the new investor of the company.

Earning price ratio

= (Earnings per share) / (Market price per share)

&

Earnings per share = (Total earning) / (Number of equity share)

It is the ratio of earning per share to market price per share and is expressed in the terms of percentage and is useful for the prospective investors in the company.

Price earnings ratio (P/E)

= (Market Price per share) / (Earnings per Share)

A high price earnings ratio indicates that investors are satisfied that the future earnings per share will increase on the other hand, a low price earnings ratio indicates that the investors are pessimistic as regards the possibility of the earnings per share to increase. From the investor point of view this ratio is of high significant. A high ratio is a sign that the share prices are relatively low in relation to recent earning per shares. It should be remembered that the purchase of a share with a high price-earnings ratio does not always imply that the investors are indulging in foolish speculation. They may be acting wisely because the ultimate performance of a share depends on the future earnings per share and not on the recent historical earnings per share. If this future earnings per share increases, the ratio may not be too high.

Price to Sales ratio

= (Current Market Price) / Annual Net Sales per shares

Or

= (Market Capitalization) / Annual Sales

A high P/S ratio indicates highly priced stock, a low P/S ratio indicate an undervalued stock. This ratio may be used along with other data and compared with similar companies in the industry.

Price to Book Value Ratio

Book Value = (Net Worth) / (Number Of Shares)

&

P/BV = (CMP) /(BV)

This ratio finds the price relative to the value, if P/BV ratio is less than it indicates the company is trading below its book value and stock is undervalued. But it should not be the only parameters while selecting stock.

Growth Adjusted Price to Earnings Ratio

PEG = { (Current Price of Stock)/(Earnings Per Share) } / (Growth Rate)

The thumb rule is that if the PEG ratio is 1, it means that the market is valuing a stock in accordance with the stock's estimated EPS growth. If the PEG ratio is less than 1, it means that EPS growth is potentially able to surpass the market current valuation and the stock price is undervalued. On the other hand, stocks with high PEG ratios can indicate just the opposite, that the stock is currently overvalued.

Profitability Ratio

Such ratio defines how profitable the operations are, though profitability can be evaluated at P&L statement. Two main parameters of profitability are EBIT Margin & PAT Margin.

EBIT Margin = EBITDA / Net Sales

These margins are useful in identifying profitability trends in an industry since it is not affected by non cash items and tax.

PAT Margin = PAT / Net Sales

A trend of increasing margins mean improving profitability which ultimately increase the shareholders worth.

Leverage Ratio

These ratio used to analyze the extent of leverage used by a business and its ability to meet the obligation arising from them. Two parameters of leverage are Debt Equity ratio and Interest coverage ratio.

Debt Equity Ratio = Long Term Debt / Net Worth.

It indicates the proportion of funds which are acquired by long term borrowings in comparison to shareholders funds. D/E ratio if 1 or less should be considered, high levels of debt in a business can prove to be detrimental.

Interest Coverage Ratio

Interest Coverage ratio = EBIT / Interest Expenses

If ratio is high, business is in comfort zone and vice versa. It means that earnings are less than interest obligation.

CHAPTER NINE

Index & Market Index

Before discussing market index, it needs to understand Index.

An index number which measure the change in a set of values over a period of time.

a. Index number are a specialized type of average
b. Index numbers study the effects of such factors which cannot be measured directly.
c. Index numbers bring out the common characteristics of a group of items.
d. The changes mentioned above can be either in relation to time or in relation to place.

TYPES OF INDEX NUMBER

Index number is classified on the basis of the phenomena whose changes they measure.

a. Price Index Number (wholesale and Retail)
b. Quantity Index Number
c. Value Index Number
d. Special purpose Index Number.

If we think of Index number and Stock Market or Market Index it may be useful in various way

i. Help in studying trend

j. Help in policy formulation
k. Help in measuring the purchasing power of money

ax. Help in deflating various values

all. Act as economic barometers.

By studying market index we could know how the market is going on, a stock index number is the current relative value of a weighted average of the prices of a pre-defined group of equities. The starting value or base of index is usually set to a number such as 100 or 1000.

A stock market index represents the market. The market goes up if the stock market thinks that the prospective dividends in the future will be better than previous, if the dividends thought is pessimistic, the index goes down. A good index is a tradeoff between diversification and liquidity.

MARKET CAPITALISATION WEIGHTED INDEX

Here, the equity price is weighted by the market capitalization of the company. Hence each constituent stock in the index affects the index value in proportion to the market value of all the outstanding shares.

PRICE WEIGHTED INDEX

It is a stock market index where each constituent makes up a fraction of the index that is proportional to its price. For a stock market index this implies that stocks are included in proportional based on their quoted prices

Apart from these two we have equal weighted index.

BSE INDEX – SENSEX

SENSEX, first complied in 1986 was calculated on a Market Capitalization Methodology of 30 components stock representing a sample of large, well established and financially sound companies. The base year of SENSEX is 1978 – 79. The index was initially calculated based on Full Market Capitalization methodology but was shifted to the Free Float Methodology with effect from 1st September 2003.

NSE INDEX – NIFTY 50

NSE IS India's largest market incorporated in the year 1992. Trading commenced in 1994. NSE provided the electronic limit order book to trade derivatives &ETFs. NSE Index NIFTY 50, includes 50 companies of the listed on the NSE. The Index has been trading since 22nd April 1996. The NIFTY 50 covers 12 sectors of the Indian economy and expose to the Indian market in one portfolio.

CHAPTER TEN

Financial Market

Financial market consists of two words viz. finance and market.

Finance

Finance is the prerequisite for business. It is the process of conversion of accumulated funds to productive use. Finance is the activity concerned with the raising and administering of funds used in business.

Market

It's a place where buyer and seller meet to facilitate the exchange of Goods and services. Market may be physical like retail outlet where buyer and seller meets or virtual market where there is no direct physical contract between the parties. Market establishes the price of goods and services that are determined by supply and demand. Market types include illegal market, auction market and financial market.

Financial market may be classified as negotiated loan market and open market.

Negotiable Loan Market – Here the lender and the borrower personally negotiate the terms of the loan agreement, e.g. borrowing from a bank.

Open Market – An impersonal market in which securities are treated in large volume. The stock market is an example of an open market.

Financial markets are again divided into two category depending upon the credit requirement for short and long term purposes viz. money market and capital market.

(A)Money Market:-

(I) Short term Debt Market

It deals with the short term lending and borrowing of funds and money market is not a place rather an activity. It is a region where short term funds are bought and sold. Money market instrument are as follow.

(i) Call Money – These loans are given for very short period not exceeding seven days under any circumstances. There is no demand of collateral securities against call money. Call Money are useful to commercial banks.

(ii) Treasury bill – The treasury bills are Government paper securities for a short period usually of 91 days, 182 days and 364 days to pay a specific sum after a specific period. These are sold by Reserve Bank of India on behalf of Government. They are issued at a discount and redeemed at par and it is a type of zero coupon bonds. The yield on treasury bills are determined through the auction process.

(iii) Commercial Paper – These are unsecured promissory notes which are issued by well reputed companies to meet the demand of short term and working capital need. These are issued for a period of 15 days to 12 months. Usually these are issued on discount but sometimes they are issued on definite rate of interest.

(iv) Certificate of Deposit – Certificate of deposits is a negotiable instrument which can be transfer after a certain period by an endorsement. It is issued by scheduled commercial banks, EXIM Banks and Financial institutions. And issued for 91 days. the face value is minimum 5 Lakhs.

(v)Commercial Bill – It is used to finance the credit sales. The seller draws the bill and the buyer accepts it. The buyer honors the bill on due date. Seller can get the bill discounted from the bank. Generally issued for a period of 90 days.

(II) Long Term Debt Market

(i) Government Securities – Government bond are also called gilts or Treasury bond and such bonds are otherwise denoted as G – Sec. These instruments are issued by Reserve Bank of India on behalf of Government. Mainly to bridge the gap of fiscal deficit such instrument are issued. Some G – Sec. are issued as zero coupon bond and others are issued as interest paying coupon bond. G – Sec. represent most liquid segment and these are traded in securities market. A separate market segment was setup with a minimum of Rs. 10000/- trading lot for retail investor. These bond do not offer tax benefit on interest and maturity value, tax will be imposed like other fixed income instrument.

(ii) Corporate Bond - Long term corporate bonds are of two types

(a) Bond issued by public sector units (PSU)

(b) Bond issued by private corporate sectors

PSU bonds are further categories into taxable and tax free bonds. Bonds which are issued by NHAI (National Highway Authority of India), NHB(National Housing Bank), NABARD(National bank for Agriculture and Rural Development), qualify for saving in capital gains. Investment in such type of bond allows saving tax on long term capital gains. Secondary market for corporate bond are illiquid.

(B)Capital Market:-

It enables long term transfer of funds using Equity or Debt instrument. It is an organized mechanism for effective and efficient transfer of money capital from investing parties to ultimate destination. And capital markets are of two types' primary market and secondary market.

(i) Primary Market:-

Where Securities are sold in the market for the first time i.e. new securities are issued from the company. In this market, it is the flow of funds from saver to borrowers and helps directly in formation of capital. It comes before secondary market. It has no particular place

(a) IPO:-

The first public offer of shares made by a company is called an Initial public offer (IPO). An IPO may be issue of fresh shares by the company or by existing shareholders like promoters or financial institution or combination of both.

(b) FPO:-

A follow on Public Offer is made by the company that already has made an IPO during past. When a company wants additional capital or for capital restructure by redeeming debt, it raise capital through fresh issue of capital in follow on Public offer.

(c) Right Shares :–

The right shares are offered to the existing investor, those who have already shares in that particular company. The shareholder has the right to accept the offer or assign his right in favor of another person.

(ii) Secondary Market:-

It is the market for the sale and purchase of previously issued or second hand securities and it leads the concept of "Stock Market". It comes after primary market and has a particular place and creates liquidity.

STOCK EXCHANGE

It is an organized market where securities issued by companies, Government organization, semi government organization are sold and purchased. Here dealing can be done only through authorized members like Broker and sub broker and it is necessary to obey the rules and bye -law. There are 24 stock exchange in India out of which Bombay Stock Exchange and National Stock Exchange are the main stock Exchange. **BSE** known as Bombay Stock Exchange is the Asia's first stock exchange, and start functioning in the year 1875. And Index is known as SENSEX, which is calculated by taking price of 30 stocks across key sector of BSE. **NSE** In the year 1992 NSE established as demutualized electronic exchange. It was the first exchange in the country to provide fully automated screen based electronic trading system. And Index is known as NIFTY, and calculated by taking prices of 50 key stock listed in NSE.

SEBI was set up in the year 1988 and start functioning in the year 1992, to ensure that stock exchange performs their self regulatory role properly, to meet the need of

- Issuer
- Investor
- Intermediaries.

Prior to SEBI, stock exchange were being supervised by the Ministry Of Finance under the Securities Contract Act (SCRA) and were operating more or less self regulatory organizations. When malpractice crept into trading and in order to protect investor interest SEBI was setup.

CHAPTER ELEVEN

Structure of Financial Market

Securities Market

Securities market consists of primary and secondary market. In primary market issuers raise capital by issuing securities to investor and secondary market facilitates trade in those securities which are already issued at primary market, through stock exchange. Primary market creates financial assets and the secondary market makes them marketable. Sale and purchase of securities are facilitated through financial intermediaries. The entire process of Sales and purchase is subject to regulatory control and supervision by **SEBI.**

SEBI, a statutory body appointed by Act of Parliament (SEBI ACT, 1992) is the chief regulator of securities market. THE SECURITIES CONTRACT REGULATION ACT, 1956 and THE DEPOSITORY ACT 1996 is administered by SEBI.

SEBI notified regulation that cover all activities and intermediaries in the securities market including stock broker, sub broker, merchant banker, registrar to an issue, share transfer agent, underwriters, portfolio managers, depository participants, custodian and etc. SEBI has been assigned the powers of recognizing and regulating the function of stock exchange.

Commodity Market

In India trade in commodities conducted in unorganized manner we can say in regional markets or mandies, only organized trading took place in cotton through the establishment of cotton trade association in 1875. During 90's commodity future exchanges have been encouraged. Globally CBOT and CME are the oldest derivative exchange where the main job was to standardize the qualities and quantities of the commodity that were traded.

The commodities market all over India is regulated by "The Forward Contracts (Regulation) Act, 1952. After introduction of derivative trading in securities during 2001, the term "securities" in Securities contracts (Regulation) Act, 1956 was amended to cover derivative contract in securities. When SEBI preview the regulation of derivatives, it appoints separate regulatory authorities for securities and commodity derivative markets. The national level multi commodity exchanges are:-

- National Board of Trade
- Multi Commodity Exchange of India
- National Commodity and Derivative Exchange of India.

SEBI merged with the Forward Market Commission on September 28, 2015 and regulates the commodities market in India. The regulator's role includes monitoring the trading conditions in the forward markets, including demand and supply and prices, and take necessary action to streamline the functioning of the market.

Foreign Exchange Market

In India Foreign exchange market has a spot market and forward market.

Spot Market – Is a public financial market in which financial instruments like currency and others are bought and sold for immediate delivery. The spot market is again consisted with Bank Segment and Merchant Segment.

Bank Segment – Inter Bank segment make market by giving quotes for buying and selling a currency.

Merchant Segment – The merchant are the price takers who buy and sell currency based on price given by the banks.

RBI publishes a reference rate for each currency. The reference rate for each currency is available for every week day.

Forward Market – A forward market is informal OTC market place that sets the price of a financial instrument or assets for future delivery.

OTC – Trading is done directly between two parties, without the supervision of an exchange.

Trading system is provided by the exchanges that allow currency derivative trading such as the NSE and the BSE. Settlement happens on last working day excluding Saturday.

Insurance Market

Insurance is a contract between two parties, where one promises the other to indemnify or make good any financial loss suffered by the latter (insured) in consideration for an amount received by way of premium. Losses cannot be compensated but can be reimbursed it and when they occurred. Insurance, from the view point of an individual, a financial arrangement whereby the individual can substitute a relatively small definite cost (premium) for a large uncertain financial loss.

The party whose loss makes the insurer pay the claim is "insured"

The consideration involved in the contract or what the insured pays to the insurer is "premium"

The contract of insurance is referred as "policy"

In Indian context, insurance can be broadly classified into two:-

(A)Life insurance

(B) General insurance.

(I) Life Insurance

It deals with the insurance of individual, groups and pension plans since 1st September 1956, transacting life insurance business in India was the exclusive privilege of the nationalized in insurance company LIC. However with the passing of the IRDA Act, 1999 the life insurance sector has been thrown open to private sector.

A life insurance policy that provides coverage for the whole of the insured's life is called whole life insurance. A policy that covers a set time period, such as five or ten years, is called term life insurance. Endowment policies are also term policies but the difference is, it pays benefits when the insured dies during the policy term and pays benefits if the insured survives the policy term. And annuity contracts promise to pay the insured a periodic payment.

PRODUCTS OF LIFE INSURANCE

(A) Term Insurance – A pure life insurance, i.e. there is no saving or profit components, if no claims has been made nothing can be received from this type of policy. Insurance premium is low and in the event of death of the insured, the sum assured will be paid to the beneficiaries.

(B) Endowment Insurance – Such types of policy have saving components and in return profits in shape of bonus are added at the time of maturity or in the event of death of the insured. Due to saving feature increase insurance premium are charged, in compare to Term Insurance. If saving force are eliminated then it may be more efficient to choose other option.

(C) Whole Life policy – As the name goes, such policies cover for entire life of the insurer, and only on the death of the insured, the sum assured is paid to the beneficiaries. Since death is certain, premium are higher.

(D) ULIP – A combination of insurance protection as well as investment in stock market. Unit Link Insurance Plan gained a lot of popularity due to its feature. As ULIP allows the insured to decide on the kind of portfolio that insurer should maintain. In the event of death, the sum assured is paid to the beneficiaries. If insured survives, then the Net Asset Value is returned. Premium paid by the Insured is divided in three parts. Expenses those are related to meeting at issuing policy. A portion towards covering the risk for life cover. After deducting the above component, the individual is given a choice of the funds where he/she wants to invest.

(E) Group Insurance – In such types of policies, plan can be purchased by groups for the benefits of group members, the cost of group plan is usually less than compare to individual plan. It's a plan which covers number of people in the same contract. A group plan can be for formal group or informal group. Formal group comprises employer-employee group, professional organization, business organization & etc. whereas informal group may belong to society or cultural association. The manger of the group gets a master policy in the name of the group. A member is covered as long as he is part of the group.

The non-life insurance or general insurance segment covers motors, health insurance travel insurance, fire and personal accident, among others. There are 28 insurance in this segment.

(II) NON LIFE INSURANCE POLICY

Other than life Insurance all insurance are covered under non life insurance. Non life insurance is otherwise known as General Insurance and it covers health insurance, motor insurance, travel insurance, accident insurance and etc. A range of general insurance products are available for different need and demand.

(A) Health Insurance – Insurance which covers for medical expenses that arises out of illness, sickness and disease, as per the sum assured. Limits for hospitalization, coverage of non-medical items, Ambulance service, pre and post hospitalization expenses, and day care treatment, home care treatment may be setup. Health Insurance can be purchased on individual or floater basis (for family under the same policy). Depending upon the policy pre existing disease are also covered after some waiting period.

(B) Travel Insurance – It covers losses made during travel and death related cost, baggage lost, lost of documents as per the policy terms and condition.

(C) Motor Insurance – In motor insurance two types of policy are there viz. Comprehensive and third party insurance. Comprehensive insurance covers the cost of motor, its accessories and cover people affected by motor accidents. Whereas in third party insurance only people affected by motor accidents are covered.

Health insurance is a contingent claim contract on the insured incurring additional expenses or losing income because of incapacity or loss of good health. Payment becomes necessary because physical or mental incapacity prevents the insured from being able to work is called disability income insurance. If the incapacity prohibits the insured's activities of daily living, it is called long term care insurance. If the insured incurs hospital, physician or other health care expenses it is called medical expense insurance. In India, only medical expense insurance is available.

Insurance is a financial arrangement for redistributing the cost of unexpected losses through a legal contract whereby an insurer agrees to compensate an insured for losses. Insurance is different from gambling and hedging. Insurance deals with existing risk and involves a transfer of pure risk.

The products are distributed through multiple channels such as agency, bancssurance, direct agents, broking and corporate agency are among them.

IRDAI regulates the insurance sector in India in accordance with the terms of the IRDA Act of 1999. IRDAI is licensing authorities for insurance company.

Pension Market

The Government pension plan has moved from defined benefit structure, where employee and employer contribution to the pension fund by "NPS". The NPS is contribution pension scheme applicable to Government employee and the Government makes matching contributions, a fund of the employee choice. NPS is also available for general public. On retirement the corpus accumulated in NPS is used to buy annuity offered by insurance companies. PFRDA is the regulator of the pension market. It is responsible for registering the various constituent like manager, custodian, and central record keeping agency and trustee banks and to define the parameters of their roles and responsibilities.

Banking Market

The function of banking system is to accept deposits and make credit available to those that qualify for it and this function of bank is generally understood fundamental banking services.

Small Saving Instruments

These schemes have the implicit guarantee of the Government such schemes are offered through post office and selected banks. Rate of interest on small savings are dynamic. Hence rate of interest on small saving instrument will be aligned with the G – Sec. rate of similar maturity and announced in April every year.

Public Provident Fund

Public Provident fund is a 15 years deposit account that can be opened with post office or designated bank. A person can hold only one PPF account. It is long term retirement plan for those individuals who may not be covered by provident funds of their employer or self employed. Minimum amount that needs to be deposited is in this account is Rs 500/- and the maximum is Rs 1,50,000/- and can be paid in one lump sum or in installment not exceeding 12 times in a financial year. One withdrawal is allowed from 7th financial year. In the event of death of the account holder the balance in the account shall be paid to the nominee or legal heir. A deduction under section 80 C of the Income Tax Act is allowed and the interest is completely tax free.

PPF account is not subject to attachment seizure of account by court order under any order or decree of a court.

National Saving Certificate

National saving certificate is issued by Government and sold at post office. NSC are issued with tenor of 5 years and 10 years. The certificate can be bought by individuals on their own account or on behalf of minor. NSC can be bought by cash or through bank the minimum investment is Rs 500/- and no maximum limit. Under section 80 C of the Income Tax Act tax benefit is there, premature encashment is allowed in case of death. Nomination is allowed in the certificates, and NSC are also accepted as collateral for taking loan.

Senior Citizen Saving Scheme

Only senior citizen of age 60 years or above can enjoy the scheme on the date of opening. The age limit is reduced to 55 years in case of individual retiring on superannuation or under VRS provided the account is opened within one month of the date of retirement. The account can be open at any post office and designated bank. The term of scheme is 5 years, maximum limit of investment is Rs 15 lakhs. Nominee facility is available here. A person can open more than one account subject to the condition, that the amount in all accounts taken together does not any point exceeds Rs 15 lakhs.

Kisan Vkias Patra

The KVP can be purchased by an adult for self or by two adults for minor investor. It can be purchased from post office or bank. The minimum investment is Rs. 1,000/- and there is no maximum limit. The facility of nomination is there and can be transferred from one person to another, premature encasement can be done but after two and half years. No tax incentive is there and interest earned is taxed on accrual basis.

Sukanya Samridhi Account Scheme

Is a scheme launched for the benefit of girl children. The account will be opened in the name of girl child by a natural or legal guardian. The account can be opened with any authorized bank, only one account can be opened in name of girl child and a parent or guardian can open maximum two accounts. The minimum investment in account is Rs 1,000/- and maximum of Rs 1.5 lakhs. The account will mature on the completion of 21 years from the date of opening of the account. Partial withdrawal is allowed after the holder attains 18 years of age, to the extent of 50% of the amount in balance at the end of allowed.

Sovereign Gold Bond Scheme

Scheme was launched to provide an alternative way for investors to take exposure to gold as an investment. SGB are government securities denominated in grams of gold. The bonds are issued in denomination of one gram of gold and in denomination thereof. The tenor of bond is 8 years, each bond investors buy in cash and on redemption are paid the maturity value in cash. The value of bond reflects price of gold. The bond is tradable on stock exchange and it can be hold in physical or dematerialized form. The minimum investment is 2 grams and maximum is 500 grams and will be taxed as per the prevalent tax laws and capital gains.

Gold Monetization Scheme

GMS is intended to mobilize the idle gold lying in household, trust and other places and facilitate its use for productive purposes and in long run to reduce country's reliance on the imports of gold. The minimum gold can be deposited under the scheme is 30 grams and there is no maximum limit. The gold can be converted into short term bank deposit (1 – 3 years) or medium term deposit (5 – 7 year) or long term bank deposit (12 – 15 years) accepted by the designated bank on behalf of the Central Government. This will earn interest at the rate fixed by the respective bank. The interest will be credited periodically to the account and can be either withdrawn or allowed to accumulate till maturity. The redemption will be made only in rupees at the prevailing value of gold at the time of redemption.

CHAPTER TWELVE

Mutual Fund

As the name mutual fund seems pool of money or fund, collected from the investors and is invested according to certain investment objectives. The contributors and beneficiary of the fund or pool of money, are the same class of people i.e. investor. As the pool of funds held by investors mutually is the mutual fund. Today there are more than 500 products in mutual fund approximately. Though we can classify mutual fund in different heads, it may also decide the manner in which their returns would be distributed, like, daily, monthly, quarterly, half yearly, yearly, reinvestment of dividend into the mutual fund product itself.

Here all funds are not invested in the same investment or we can say the funds are invested in different sectors as risk and return of various sector options do not move uniformly, if the IT sector is going down, then then the Iron and Steel sector may move up. If the equity market is moving up, then debt market may move down. Thus if diversified portfolio is there, then risk can be managed.

Product

Usually mutual fund denominated in units, created by pooling investor contribution. Depending upon the nature of participation and nature of income of income distribution we on classify the choice of investor

A. Nature Of Participants

a. Open – Ended -à In open ended investors can buy and sell units of the fund, at NAV related prices, at any time directly from the fund.
b. Closed – Ended -à A closed ended fund is open for sale to investors for a specific period, after which further sales are closed. Any further transaction for buying the units or repurchasing them happens in secondary markets, where closed end funds are listed.

A. Nature of income distribution

c. Dividend Option – In dividend option investor will receive dividends from the mutual fund when dividends are declared.
d. Growth option – In growth option income earned are retained in the investment portfolio and allowed to grow further.

REGULATORY STRUCTURE

Mutual fund in India is governed by SEBI (Mutual Fund) Regulations, 1996. Thus as per regulation, it is mandatory for mutual funds to have a three tire structure of sponsor – Trustee – Assets management company (AMC).

I. Sponsor – Is the promoter of the mutual fund, and appoints trustee.
II. Trustee – Are responsible to the investor in the mutual fund, and appoint the AMC.
III. AMC – For managing the investment portfolio.

Both the mutual fund and AMC have to be registered with SEBI.

PROCESS

In the prescribed format mutual fund is required to provide information about the fund and the scheme. This document is called prospectus or offer document or key information memorandum. It contains all relevant information that an investor would need. In case of closed end fund, the offer document is issued during the IPO's. In case of the open ended scheme offer document is valid through the life of the scheme, and is required to be revised at least once in 2 years.

Generally investor buys units of a mutual fund. For example, a mutual fund scheme usually offer unit at a price of Rs. 10/- . If investor wanting to invest Rs. 5000/- in this scheme will buy 500 units.

An existing mutual fund scheme announced the mutual fund every day and is based on the NAV of the fund.

PRODUCTS OF MUTUAL FUNDs

Though diversified portfolios, mutual funds enables investing in various assets classes, the risk of an investor is lower than directly investing in securities due to diversify portfolio.

(A) Equity Funds – Funds those are invested in equity instrument, such funds are created with an objective of generating long term growth and capital appreciation. While investing in this fund stock are further classified on the basis of Capital & Industry. Like large capital, medium capital, small capital, sector funds. Funds performance depends upon the investment universe and the strategies adopted.

(B) Debt Fund- Funds made up with various types of debt securities. Debt securities may be short term, medium term, or long term. Debts Fund have two source of income coupon and capital gains. Coupon is the interest income whereas the capital gain arise only in such condition, with the change in market rates, if interest rate fall the value of the Debt securities go up and vice versa.

(C) Hybrid Fund – Fund provide investors a diversified portfolio in a single bucket. Fund invests in more than one class i.e. Debt and Equity depending on the investment objectives.

(D) Equity Link Saving Schemes – It is a special category of diversified equity funds with a lock in period of minimum three years. By investing in ELSS fund investor get dual benefits of tax deductions and wealth accumulation over time. Investor can enjoys a tax deduction under section 80C of the Income Tax Act.

(E) Index Fund – In such funds, Fund manager need not pay any active role, while selecting industries and stocks to build portfolio. It is a passive investment strategies, Fund manager copies the Index while building the fund's portfolio. If the weight of any stock changes within Index, Fund manager must sell or buy units of stock accordingly.

(F) Electronic Traded Funds – It is an Exchange traded fund like a common stock on a stock exchange. This fund is linked to an underlying index, but must be listed and traded on a stock exchange. It has lower fees and higher liquidity than mutual funds. Investor needs a Demat Account to deal in the unit.

(G) Money Market Fund – Such funds invested in highly liquid instrument, short term debt securities with very low level of risk. It includes cash and cash equivalent securities.

(H) Aggressive Growth Fund – This funds operates on the principle high risk high rewards. Such fund seeks capital gain by investing in the shares of growth company stock. Such funds have a chance of sudden growth as well as have same level of risk factors.

(I) Capital Protection Fund – The prime objective of this fund is to protect investor's capital during market down turns. It's closed ended hybrid fund with a view focus on debt to achieve capital protection. Allocation between equity and debt is based on the terms of the scheme.

Purchase of Mutual fund units

Net Asset Value (NAV) determines the price for the shares in a mutual fund calculated after the market closes. And NAV is calculated in unit price of a mutual fund scheme, the NAV is determined on daily basis. NAV is calculated by dividing the total value of all the cash and securities in the portfolio minus liability if any by the number of outstanding share.

NAV = {(value of all cash and securities) – (liability)} / (Number of shares).

An investor can make an initial investment in mutual fund either in the New Fund Offer (NFO) or when the open ended fund opens for transaction for fresh purchase of units.

(A) Purchase of units in NFO – NFO can be purchased by an investor in the units of any mutual fund scheme during the pre defined period and may subscribe to the NFO at an offer price. NFO is a fund on first subscription basis for financing its purchase of securities. It is usually fixed at Rs. 10/- , after the tenure expire the investor would be able to purchase at NAV or redeem investment. The folio number is created at the time of the allotment and is unique identity of the investor.

(B) Purchase in continuous offer period – Once the scheme opens for transaction, investor can buy additional units or redeem. At the time of fresh allotment folio number is created under which all information related to the investor are recorded as per regulatory compliance and KYC (know your Client) norms. Additional investments are added in existing folio number. Investor can invest directly in a mutual fund by choosing Direct Plan option at any AMC (Asset Management Company) official point of acceptance or through the mutual fund advisor registered with AMFI.

(C) Redemption of mutual fund – In open ended scheme of mutual fund, fund can be realized at any time by redeeming the units. A redemption request can be made for all the units held or part of it. The redemption request can specify the amount or number of units to be redeemed. However mutual fund may specify the minimum redemption amount of each transaction.

(D)Systematic Transaction – systematic transaction plan let the investor to commit to a set of transaction in advance, the value of each investment, the day of transaction and the periodicity of the transaction may be decided at the time of commitment. The transaction will be executed at the applicable NAV at the time of execution. Initiated systematic transaction can be cancelled at any time by the investor after giving due notice.

(i) Systematic Investment Plan – Here investor commit to invest a fixed amount at regular interval over a period of time. Investment is made at different prices over the term chosen and allows investor benefit from the volatility in the market. The same amount being invested in each investment, investor buy more units when the price is low and less units when the price is high, as a result cost of acquisition per unit comes down. This is cost of acquisition averaging. And by this SIP provides advantage to the investor. Investor can make additional investment in his existing folio. If a fresh investment is made a folio is created with the SIP enrolment. The number of unit in each investment can be accumulated in the same folio either NFO or otherwise. A SIP can be discontinue or cancelled at any point of time. However before enrolling SIP an investor must make decision like the scheme, plan and option, the amount to be invested in each period, terms of the investment, date and the tenor of the plan.

(ii) Systematic Withdrawal Plan – In such plan an investor from the balance held in mutual fund investment can structure a regular pay out by registering SWP. Investors have the option to choose the amount and frequency of withdrawal. At the set date, units from the portfolio are sold and the funds are transferred to account. Investor can either withdraw a fixed amount or only the capital appreciations. SWP is redemption from a scheme, the redemption amount will be credited to the Bank Account registered with the mutual fund. SWP will close if the balance in folio falls below a specified amount, investor can cancelled a SWP at any point of time.

(iii) Systematic Transfer Plan – This plan allow investor to shift their investment from one scheme to the other without any hassles. It's a process of fund transfer in a streamline which is the primary advantages of the investor.

(iv) Switch – A switch is a single transfer from one scheme or option of a scheme to another scheme. In a switch an investor can transfer all or portion of the funds held in investment. The investor must specify the source and target schemes and option and the amount to be switched.

Taxation of Mutual Fund

Returns from mutual fund in shape of value appreciation, interest and dividends belong to the investor, the returns received by the investor in which ever form are considered as capital gains after deducting the actual amount invested in the fund. When the units are redeemed such returns are taxable in the hand of investor. However taxable amount can be trace only after considering the nature of investment, period of investment holding and the type of investor. Depending upon the holding period of the investment before redemption are determined in order to categorize the gains as short or long term capital gains. If the units are hold for less than 12 months, it is considered to be short term capital gain and if the holding is more than 12 months it is considered long term capital gain. Indexation process of calculation is applied while calculating long term capital gains, after adjusting the purchase price. Investor can enhance post tax returns by choosing the right investment. Mutual fund offers investment option, how investor should take the return from the investment so as to plan the taxation. It offers a dividend option and growth option, there is a dividend reinvestment option too where dividends are not paid and it got reinvested again. The need of periodic income can be met by using periodic redemption and by this the capital gains tax will be lower. Most of the fund do not impose exit load if investment is held for a minimum period, depending upon the types of scheme.

CHAPTER THIRTEEN

Commonly Used Terms In Stock Market

A. **Averaging**

Buying shares at different prices, quantity and time, for advantageous average price. For example: - some has bought 100 shares at Rs. 70/- in a rising market, when the price falls to Rs. 50/- he may buy another 200 shares. By averaging he has obtained a price of Rs. 40/- for a share. He may still buy further shares when the price is lower, by averaging he may obtain an even lower price. Averaging is often done to offset the high price once paid in a rising market.

A. **Bear Market**

A stock market dealer who expects share prices to fall and keep selling (to pick up the shares, later a lower price), causing selling pressure and lowering the prices further. Term derived from the attacking posture of the bear, pushing down wards.

(c) Bull Market

A dealer who believes that share prices are going to rise and keeps buying to sell latter at a profit. Term derived from attacking posture of the bull, giving an upward thrust, the bulls action causes buying pressure in the market place and pushes up share prices.

(D) Profit Booking

Making profit by selling shares which has gone above its purchase price. When shares, which an investor holds, go up in price the investor has made only notional profit, which is meaningless. He makes profit only when he sells them, he does make profit.

(E) Blue Chip

Shares of particularly well known and established companies which have shown consistent growth over the years, have bright future prospects, and are expected to continue sustained growth in the future. The word derived from casino gambling where the blue chip is usually the one with the highest value.

(F) Correction

A sharp reversal, usually downwards in the price of an individual share or shares. In general corrections usually occur during any long term move upwards or downwards as share prices seldom move straight up or down.

(G) Book Closer

Before a company declares a dividend or issues bonus or right share, it closes it register of members for a certain period, from one week to a month during which no transfer of shares is registered. Only those shareholders whose names appear on the register after the book closure are eligible to receive dividends and bonus and entitlement to right shares.

(H) **Record Date**

For the purposes of dividend distribution and entitlement to bonus or right share issue, a company fixes a date on which a shareholder must officially own shares to qualify. If a share has changed hands after the declaration of dividend, bonus or right before this date but the transfer has not been entered in the register of the company, the transferee can get the benefit of the dividend etc., only through the stock broker.

(I) No Delivery Period

Whenever a book closure or a record date is announced by a no delivery period for that security. During this period, trading is permitted in the security. However, these trades are settled only after no delivery period.

(J) Portfolio

Combined holding of many kinds of financial securities, shares, debentures, government bond, mutual funds and other financial assets. Making portfolio is putting ones egg in different basket with varying elements of risk and return. Reducing risk by diversification and maximization of profit.

(K) Split

During distribution of bonus shares through which the ownership value of each existing share is split. A split also occurs when a company decides to reduce the par value of a share by issuing a proportionate number of lower value shares. When a Rs.100/-share is split and 10 shares of Rs. 10 are issued in exchange.

(L) Volatile

Is subject to frequent and violent fluctuation. If the volatility of a share is due to inherent factors like variability in its earnings, smallness of the issue, the cyclical nature of the industry to which it belongs, it is measured by alpha factor. If on the other hand, the volatility is market related, it is measured by the beta factor. Shares which are subject to sharp fluctuation in price showing a considerable difference between their highest and lowest recorded prices.

(M) ISIN International Securities Identification Number.

SEBI being the national number agency for India has permitted NSDL for Demat shares.

While allotting ISINs, NSDL observe that:-

i. The ISINs allotted by NSDL does not at any point of time breach the uniqueness of ISIN of physical form for the same security.
ii. ISIN for a security is allotted only when the security is admitted to NSDL.
iii. The numbering system is simple.
iv. The numbering system of ISIN is in compliance with the structure of ISIN adopted by SEBI.

The numbering structure for securities in NSDL is of 12 digit alpha numeric string.

(N) Financial Institution (FI)

Government and public corporations like LIC, HDFC, ICICI, ABSL and other mutual funds with large investable resources which operate in the stock market, often beneficially by buying large chunks of share when the prices are falling, generally providing supports to the market. They also support to new public issues IPOs. The presence of the FIs in the stock market has been responsible for the market behaving in a fairly steady to fashion.

(O)Foreign Institutional Investor (FIIs)

FIIs refer to outside entities investing in a country outside of the one in which it is registered. All FIIs in India must register themselves with SEBI to participate in the market. FIIs are allowed to invest in India's Primary and Secondary markets and allow FIIs to purchase shares and debentures.

(P) Hedging

In the investment of one's fund in the stock market, it is done by different kind of shares, so that if one falls in price another will rise, or investing in different kinds of assets e.g. shares debenture bonds gold and silver real estate etc. Hedging against inflation is putting ones money on assets which will neutralize inflationary increases. A perfect hedge is a no risk no gain precaution.

(Q)Large Cap and Small Cap

The size of a company in the equity market is determined by the number of shares issued by the company. The market price, at which shares are traded. This number (number of share issued x market price per share) is called as market capitalization.

If the market capitalization of a company is high, we call such a company as a large cap company. Higher the market capitalization, greater the liquidity in the stock market.

Companies which are closely held or are very small, tend to have a smaller market capitalization. These are called small cap companies.

(R) **Cyclical Stock**

If the earnings of a company are subject to ups and downs over years, caused mostly due to cyclical changes in economic variables such stock are called as cyclical stocks.

(S) Growth Stock

Growth stocks belong to those sectors which have the potential for higher earnings. These are typical sectors which are new and therefore have a potential for high profits to early entrants.

(T)Value Stock

Value stocks are those that have an established earnings history, but tends to be undervalued in the market for brief period.

(U) Stock Broker

A broker is an intermediary who arranges to buy and sell securities on behalf of client (the buyer and seller). A stock broker applies for registration to SEBI through a stock exchange or stock exchanges of which he or she is admitted as member, SEBI may grant a certificate to a stock broker.

(V) Sub Broker

A sub broker is a person who intermediates between investor and stock brokers. A sub broker acts on behalf of stock broker as an agent or otherwise for assisting the investor for buying, selling or dealing in securities through such stock broker. No sub broker is allowed to buy, sell or deal in securities unless he or she holds a certificate of registration granted by SEBI.

(W) Contract Note

A contract note is a confirmation of trades done on a particular day for and on behalf of a client. Contract note consist of all relevant details as required therein to be filled. A contract note shall be issued to a client within 24 hours of execution of the contract duly sign by trading member or authorized signatories or client attorney.

CHAPTER FOURTEEN

Recent Trend In Stock Market

Gone are the days where trading took placed in traditional method i.e. share transfer certificate and etc. Now a day a nationwide on line fully automated screen based trading system is in operation. This technology carried the trading platform from the trading hall of stock exchanges to the premises of brokers and sub brokers and further to the PCs at the residence of investors, and at the hand by using mobile through internet.

The trading system operates on a strict time and price priority. The trading system provides flexibility to the users in terms of kinds of order that can be placed on system. It provides complete market information. All quantity fields are in units and prices are quoted in Indian rupees, even clearing and settlement mechanism in Indian Securities market had changed. The stock exchanges in India were following T+2 (Trading day + 2 working day) rolling settlement for all securities. The members receive the funds / securities in accordance with the pay-in/pay-out schedule notified by respective exchange. As after setting up of the clearing corporation, the market has full confidence that settlements will take place on time and will be completed irrespective of possible default by isolated trading members. Clearing agency empanelled selected banks for electronic transfer of funds. The clearing agency forwards fund obligations file to clearing banks which, in turn debit the accounts of member and credit the account of the clearing agency. Trading platform is provided by NSE (National Stock Exchange) and BSE (Bombay Stock Exchange), the NSCCL (National Securities Clearing Corporation Ltd.), determines the fund/securities obligations of the trading member and ensures that trading meet their obligation. NSCCL becomes the legal counterparty to the net settlement obligations of every member. NSCCL is obligated to meet all settlement obligations, regardless of member defaults, without any discretion. Once a member fails on any obligations, NSCCL immediately cuts off trading and initiate recovery.

The Clearing Banks and Depositories provides the necessary interface between the Custodians/ Clearing members (Who clear for the trading members or their own transactions) for settlement of funds and securities obligations of trading members. NSCCL, with the help of Clearing Member, Custodians, Clearing Bank and Depositories settle the trades executed on exchange. However during settlement two kinds of risk may arise

(i) Counter party Risk

(ii) System Risk

(i)Counterparty Risk – This arises if parties do not discharge their obligation when due or at any time thereafter. It got two components.

a. Replacement Risk – This arises from the failure of one of the parties to transaction.

b. Principle Risk – This arises if a party discharges his obligations but the counterparties default. The seller/ buyer of the securities suffers this risk when he delivers/make payments, but does not receive payment /delivery.

(ii) System Risk – This comprises of operational, legal and systemic risk. The domino effect of successive failures can cause a failure of the settlement system.

All trades concluded during a particular trading period are settled together. A multilateral netting procedure is adopted to determine the net settlement obligations (delivery/ receipt positions) of Clearing Members on the securities pay-in-day, delivering members are required to bring in securities to NSCCL. On pay out day the securities are delivered to the respective receiving members. Settlement is deemed to be completed upon declaration and release of pay out of funds and securities. For settlement purpose members are required to open accounts with depository participants of both the depositories, NSDL (National Securities depositories Ltd.) and CDSL (Central Securities Depositories Ltd.), and every Clearing member is required to maintain and operate a clearing account with any one of the empanelled Clearing Banks at the designated Clearing Bank branches. The Clearing account is to be used exclusively for clearing and settlement operations.

MARKET INTERMEDIARIES

A. Stock Exchange –It provide a trading platform through electronic trading terminals which feature order matching by buyer and seller. Stock Exchange NSE, BSE is nationwide exchange. Stock Exchange also appoints various other agencies for settlement like clearing bank, clearing and settlement agencies.

B. Broker - A broker is an intermediary who arranges to buy and sell securities on behalf of client (the buyer and seller). A stock broker applies for registration to SEBI through a stock exchange or stock exchanges of which he or she is admitted as member, SEBI may grant a certificate to a stock broker

C. Sub Broker - A sub broker is a person who intermediates between investor and stock brokers. A sub broker acts on behalf of stock broker as an agent or otherwise for assisting the investor for buying, selling or dealing in securities through such stock broker. No sub broker is allowed to buy, sell or deal in securities unless he or she holds a certificate of registration granted by SEBI.

D. Depositories – There are two depositories in India NSDL (National Securities Depositories Limited) and CDSL (Central Depositories Security Limited). A depositories is a security (share, debenture, bond, mutual fund unit) Bank. It is a place where dematerialized physical securities are held in custody in electronic form. It provides service related to transactions in the securities held in dematerialized form, through Depository Participants.

E. Depository Participants. – Depository Participant are appointed by Depositories with the prior approval of SEBI. DP is an agent of the Depositories and is authorized to offer Depositories Services to investor. Any investor wants to trade in Stock market needs to open a Demat Account, can open through DP. Stock broker, financial institution, custodian etc. can become a Depository Participant.

F. Demat Account – It's an account where investor hold shares and other securities in an electronic format, otherwise it is known as Dematerialized Account. One cannot trade in stock market without Demat Account, if anyone having physical securities it need to get dematerialized as procedure laid by SEBI. Then only can transact such shares.

G. Custodian – Are responsible to hold funds and securities in electronic form on behalf of the owner. Apart from safeguarding securities a Custodian settles transactions with such securities. Custodian keep the client informed of the action taken on his/her behalf.

H. Clearing Corporation – CC ensure member on the stock exchange meet their obligation to deliver funds or securities and transaction are made promptly and efficient manner in handling the settlement process and delivery of transaction.

A. Clearing Bank – Clearing is the process where financial transaction are settled. Clearing Bank is an important intermediary between Clearing Corporation and Clearing Members. Every clearing member need to maintain an account with the clearing bank. In case of pay in its clearing members responsibility to make sure that funds available. In case of pay out clearing members receive in exchange of securities.

J. Merchant Bankers – Provide a number of services including management of securities issues in primary market, portfolio services, underwriting of capital issue, etc. In a new issue they evaluate the capital needs of the issuer & structure an appropriate instrument. The Merchant Bankers offer services for a fee. The Merchant Banker mainly deal in new issue and acts as a Issue Manager and Lead Manager.

K. Underwriter – Underwriter undertake the responsibility or giving a guarantee that the securities (shares and debentures) offered to the public will be subscribed for in the primary market, the firm which undertake the guarantee are called underwriter.

CHAPTER FIFTEEN

Future & Option

Before discussing future or option, let's try to understand what Forward Contract's is; it is an agreement to buy or sell an asset on a specified date and price. Here one party agrees to buy the underlying asset on a specified date and price and the other party agrees to sell the underlying asset on the same date and price. Other contract details, like delivery date price and quantity are negotiated bilaterally by the parties to the contract. However, Forward contract got several problems worldwide like lack of centralization of trading, illiquidity, counterparty risk and etc. To overcome these difficulties future markets were designed to solve the problems those exist in forward market.

A Futures contract is an agreement between two parties to buy or sell an asset at a certain time in the future at certain price, which are standardized and exchange traded. In future contract it may be offset prior to maturity by entering into an equal and opposite transaction. The standardized items are

i. Quantity of the underlying
ii. Quality of the underlying
iii. The date and month of delivery
iv. The units of price quotation and minimum price change

v. Location of settlement.

Options are the right to buy or sell a share or commodities at a certain price on a specified future date basically there are two types of options

i. **CALL OPTION** –A call option gives the right to buy an underlying assets at a specified price within a specified time period.
ii. **PUT OPTION** – A put option gives the right but not the obligation, to sell a stock at specific price by a specific time at the option expiration

TERMINOLOGY USED IN F&O

(i) Future Price – The price at which the futures contract trades in the future market

(ii) Contract Cycle – The period over which a contract trades. The index futures contracts on the NSE have one month two month and three month expiry cycle which expire on the last Thursday of the month.

(iii) Initial Margin – The amount that must be deposited in the margin Accounts at the time a future contract is first entered into is known as initial margin.

(iv) Marking To Market – At the end of each trading day, the margin account adjusted to reflect the investors gain or loss depending upon the future closing price. This is (MTM).

(v) Maintence Margin – This is set to ensure that the balance in the margin account never becomes negatives.

(v) Index option – Some options are American while other are Europeans

a. American options – That can be exercised at any time up to the expiration date most exchanges traded options are American.
b. European – That can be exercised only on the expiration date itself.

(vi) Stock Option – Option an individual stock.

(vii) Strike Price – The price specified in the options contract is known as the strike price or the exercise price.

(viii) Option Price – It is the price which the option buyer pays to option buyer pays to option seller. It is also referred to as the option premium.

Future Pricing:-

For the cost of carry model the price of the contract is defined as

F = S + C

Where

F= future price

S= spot price

C= holding cost or carrying cost

It can be expressed as

F = S (1+r) t

R = cost of financing.

There are eight basic models of trading on the Index market:-

(A)Hedging

(i) Long Securities, Short Index Future

(ii) Short Securities, Long Index Future

(iii) Have Portfolio, Short Index Future

(iv)Have Funds, Long Index Future

(B) Speculation

(v) Bullish Index, Long Index Future

(vi) Bearish Index, Short Index Future

(C) Arbitrage

(vii) Have Funds, Lend them to Market

(viii) Have Securities, Lend them to the Market.

Hedging

Does not remove losses, using hedging is the removal of unwanted exposure i.e. unnecessary risk. The hedged position will make fewer profits than the unhedged position, half the time. One should not enter into a hedging strategy hoping to make excess profits for sure; all that can come out of hedging is reduce risk.

(i) Long Securities, Short Index Futures:-

A Stock picker, purchase security, assuming that they are worth more than the market price, here there may be two kinds of risk.

- Understanding may be wrong and the company is not worth more than the market price.
- The entire market moves against him and generates losses even though the idea was correct.

The second outcome happens all the time. Every buy position on a security is simultaneously a buy position on Index, There is a simple way out "Every time one adopt a long position on a security, one should sell some amount of Index Futures.

(ii) Short Security, Long Index Futures

Similarly every sell position on a security is simultaneously a sell position on Index. Thus for simple way out every time one adopt a short position on a security, one should buy some amount of Index future.

(iii) Have Portfolio, Short Index Futures

As there is always fluctuation in share market, a person owing portfolio may have view that security price will fall in near future. During volatility, stockholder have no other option rather than to panic selling.

(iv) Have Fund, Buy Index Future.

(B) Speculation

(v) Bullish Index, Long Index Future

When for one reason or other, like good corporate result, good budget or stable Govt. whatever, one can benefited from up going Index.

- Buy selected liquid stock, which move with the index, sell them at a later date.
- Buy the Index portfolio and then sell it at a later date.

The first alternative is widely used where the second alternative is cumbersome and expensive. If the Index raises the stock picker gains and loss occurs when the Index fall.

(vi) Bearish Index, Short Index

When the market fall there are two choices:-

- Sell selected liquid securities, which move with the index and buy them at a later date.
- Sell the entire Index portfolio and then buy it at a later date.

The first alternative is widely used and the second alternative is hard to implement, if the Index falls, the stock picker's gains and losses if the Index rises.

A. **Arbitrage**

- Have Funds, Lend them to the market.
- Have Securities, Lend them to the market.

However, these practices do not exist in India.

USING INDEX OPTIONS

A. **Hedging**

(i) Having portfolio, Buy Put

An owner of portfolio may think that stock prices will fall in the near future, a way to protect portfolio from downside due to a market drop, is to buy insurance. When the index falls portfolio will lose value and the put option bought will gain, ensuring that the value of portfolio does not fall below a particular level, this level depends on the strike price of the options. By buying puts, the fund can limit its downside in case of a market fall.

C. **Speculation**

(ii) Bullish Index, Buy Index calls or sell Index puts.

If after a good corporate result, stable Govt. or good budget to get benefit from upward movement of market we have two choices.

- Buy call option on the Index
- Sell Put option on the Index

The down side to the buyer of the call option is limited to the option premium he pay for buying the option and on the other hand upside potential is unlimited the writer of put, face a limited upside and unlimited downside. If the index the Index does rise, the buyer of the put will let the option expire and will earn the premium. If an upward movement in the market proves to be wrong and the Index actually falls, then losses directly increase with the falling

Index.

(iii) Bearish Index, Sell Index call or buy Index put

Due to poor corporate result or instability of Govt. people feel that the Index would go down. We have two alternatives.

- Sell call option on the Index or
- Buy put option on the Index.

The upside to the writer of the call option is limited to the option premium he receives upright for writing the option. His downside however is unlimited. Here even if a put is purchase an unlimited upside but a limited downside. If the Index does fall profit to the extent the Index falls below the strike of put purchased. But if market goes up; all one lose is the option premium.

(iv) Anticipate Volatility; Buy a call and a put

When the market is volatile, during budget time or political uncertainty what would have to do:-

- Buy Call option on the Index at a strike K and maturity T
- Buy put option on the Index at the same strike K and of maturity T.

Combination of option is also known as straddle.

(v) Bull spreads – Buy a call and sell another.

A spread trading strategy involves taking a position in two or more options of the same type that is two or more calls or two or more puts. A spread is designed to profit if the price goes up is called a bull spread. This is basically done utilizing two call options having the same expiration date, but different exercise price. The buyer of a bull spread buys a call with an exercise price below the current Index level and sells a call option with an exercise above the current Index level. The spread is a bull spread because the trader hopes to profit from a rise in the Index. The trade is a spread because it involves buying one option and selling a related option.

(vi) Bear Spread – sell a Call and Buy another.

If the market is supposed to fall in next two month, thus to limit down side. A spread trading strategy involves taking a position in two or more options of the same type, which are two or more calls or two or more puts. A spread that is designed to profit if the price goes down is called a bear spread. This is done utilizing two call option having the same expiration date, but different exercise price. The strike price of the option purchased is greater than strike price of the option sold. The buyer of a bear spread buys a call with an exercise price above the current Index level and sells a call option with an exercise price below the current Index level.

D. **Arbitrage**

(vi) Put call parity violation
(vii) Beyond option price bounds.

CHAPTER SIXTEEN

Commodity Market

In India trade in commodities conducted in unorganized manner we can say in regional markets or mandies; only organized trading took place in cotton through the establishment of cotton trade association in 1875. During 90's commodity future exchanges have been encouraged. Globally CBOT and CME are the oldest derivative exchange where the main job was to standardize the qualities and quantities of the commodity that were traded.

The commodities market all over India is regulated by "The Forward Contracts (Regulation) Act, 1952. After introduction of derivative trading in securities during 2001, the term "securities" in Securities contracts (Regulation) Act, 1956 was amended to cover derivative contract in securities. When SEBI preview the regulation of derivatives, it appoints separate regulatory authorities for securities and commodity derivative markets. The national level multi commodity exchanges are:-

National Board of Trade

Multi Commodity Exchange of India

National Commodity and Derivative Exchange of India

Those who participate in derivative markets can be classified as

(a) Speculators – Speculators are those who wish to bet on future movements in the price of an asset.

(b) Hedger – Hedger faces risk associated with the price of an assets

(c) Arbitragers – Those who makes profit out of the discrepancy between price of the same product across different market,

As we know, trading clearing and settlement are three components of all markets.

(I) Trading

A fully automated screen based trading which supports an order driven market and totally transparent, on order driven market is that where order match on the basis of its time, price, quantity and commodity. The exchange specifies the unit of trading as well as the regular lot size and tick size for each contract traded time to time. When any order enters the trading system, it tries to find a match, if it got the match, trade is generated. Time stamping is done for accuracy and transparency. Commodity futures contracts have one month two month and three month expiry cycles.

(II) Clearing

NSCCL Undertake the responsibility to clearing of trades. NSCCL guarantee fund is maintained and managed. Clearing members including professional clearing members are entitled to clear and settle contracts through the clearing house.

(III) Settlement

Two types of settlements are there

(a) MTM (Marking to Market)

(b) Final settlement.

MTM settlement happen on a continuous basis at the end of each day in this deals are settled in cash by debiting/

crediting the clearing accounts of CM with the respective Bank. Final settlement took place on the date of expiry; the responsibility of settlement is on trading cum clearing member for trade done on his own account and his client trades. A professional clearing member is responsible for setting all the participants trades which he has confirmed to the exchange. At last member submit delivery information through delivery request window on the trader's workstation for all open position and all constituents individually.

Due to hedging, speculation and arbitrage derivatives become popular. Now a days future and option are traded on many exchange, where as forward contract are popular on the OTC market.

Forward contracts in an agreement to buy or sell assets on a specified date for a specified price. One of the party may agrees to buy the assets assumes a long position the other party may agrees to sell the assets assumes a short position on a certain specific future date for a certain specified price. Other contract details like date of delivery, price, quality, quantity etc. are negotiated bilaterally by the parties to the contract. Forward contracts are normally traded outside the exchange.

FUTURE

A future contract is an agreement between two parties to buy or sell on asset of certain time in future at a certain price, future contracts are exchange traded. There are certain specific standard features to facilitate liquidity in future contracts. Future contract may be offset prior to maturity by entering into an equal and opposite transactions.

OPTION

An option gives the holder of the option the right to do something. The holder does not have to exercise this right. The purchase of an option requires on upfront payment which we can say in other words premium. Basically there are two types of option

(i) Call – call option gives the holder the right but not the obligation to buy an asset by a certain date for a certain price.

(ii) Put – put option gives the holder the right but not the obligation to sell an assets by a certain date for a certain price.

FUTURE PRICING

Future exchange act as a point of statistics on supply, transportation, purchases, exports, imports, currency value etc. Any significant changes in this data is immediately reflect in trading, due to new information trader adjust their bid and offer accordingly. As a result the market determines the best estimated price for today and tomorrow. Considering the demand and supply for the underlying commodity.

For pricing, let's looks at cost-of-carrying model.

If a buyer, buying the assets today in the spot market and holding it, then it incurs cash outlay and storing cost. Instead if the buyer buys the assets in forward market, he does not incur an initial outlay. Here the cost of holding is incurred by the seller.

This form the basis for the cost of carry model where the price of the futures contract is defined as

F= S+C

Where

F= future price

S= spot price

C=holding cost

The fair value of a future contract can be expressed as
F=(1+r)t
r = percent cost financing
t= time till expiration

MARGIN

Margin differs from commodity to commodity depends upon the changes in prices and volatility, normally margin is between 10-15% of the contract value. Margin in commodities is calculated in VaR system.

DELIVERY OF COMMODITY

It is not mandatory to take delivery, but there is a provision for delivering in commodity future trading. However the buyer and seller have to express his intention for delivery. Provision varies from exchange to exchange. The contracts which are not assigned for delivery will be settled in cash. Actual delivery has to be made in terms of the delivery units notified by the exchange.

CHAPTER SEVENTEEN

Foreign Market

The foreign exchange market is otherwise known as Currency market. The growth in international trade resulted in evolution of Foreign Exchange, as everything cannot be produced by each country. When there is a cross border trade, there is need to determine the price of different currencies in terms of one another in order to enable trade between countries. The legal framework for the conduct of foreign exchange transactions in India is provided by the Foreign Management Act, 1999. Foreign exchange transactions in India happens both on an OTC market and an exchange traded market. The Foreign exchange market has a spot market where currency is transacted for immediate settlement and a derivative market where the transactions are settled at a future date. The concept of a 24 hours market becomes true. Around the world, business hours overlap as some centers close, others open and begin to trade. The exchange rates of major currencies tend to be virtually same in all the financial centers, where there is active trading. The most significant part of currency market is the concept of currency pairs. While initiating a trade one must buy one currency and sell another currency. Thus same currency has different value against every other currency. Hence we need to identify the two currencies in a trade by giving them name. The two currency are called Base Currency (BC) and Quoting currency (QC). The BC is the currency that is priced and its amount is fixed at one units. The other currency is the QC which price the BC and its amount varies as the price of BC varies in the market. The standard practice is to write the BC code first followed by the QC code. The principle participants in Foreign exchange market are the Authorized Dealer (AD), foreign exchange brokers and customers. The authorized dealers are the market makers who give buy and sell quotes for different currency pairs. The broker act as intermediaries who find the best quotes for their clients who may be the end users of the currency.

Market Segment

(A) OTC Spot Market

It consists of two segments Interbank Foreign Exchange Market and Merchant Foreign Exchange Market. Interbank is a market where financial institution mainly Banks trade currency and other currencies derivative among themselves. It is a global network and the largest segment in the spot market. The bank quotes price for both buying and selling the currency, it is called market making. Bank as a market maker gives two way quotes viz. bid price for buying and ask price for selling. The interbank rate forms the basis for pricing large value transaction. The trades form the base for the currency exchange rates, the market ensures a fair and close spread. In the Merchant market, merchant are price takers and banks are price givers. Merchant may ask banks to quote two way prices as such merchant may have both side interest, to sell or buy and both.

(B) Settlement Dates and Value Dates

The settlement of transactions done in the spot market happens on gross settlement basis, the process of settlement where participants exchange the goods traded on the maturity of contract is called as gross settlement and where participant only settle the difference in value of goods is net settlement. The date of settlement of a spot transaction is called spot value date and it is different from the trade date. The trade date is the date on which the terms of transaction, such as price, amount, currency and value date are agreed upon by the parties to the transaction. Value date is the spot date, which may be after two business days as settlement take place in two different centers subject to both centers being open on that day. If either of the centres is closed, then the next business day when both centers are open will be fixed as the value date of transaction. It is however possible to settle the transaction before spot date. But the price at which the settlement takes before spot date will be a derived price. Spot date is at T+2 and if settlement happens on the trade date then the settlement price is called cash.

(C)Currency Derivative Market

Derivative derives their value from the underlying assets. And currency derivatives are financial contracts which includes future, option and swap and such instruments have no value of their own, they derive it from the spot currency prices. Derivative contracts are those that traded today but settled at a date in future. The primary function of the derivative market is to enable risk transfer by providing a way to hedge the currency arising from a transaction.

(D) OTC Derivative Market

Small companies that lack resources to be listed on formal exchange are traded at OTC. It comprises a wide range of financial instrument like stock, debt securities and derivatives. OTC a decentralized place with no physical location, OTC trading is done through dealer network. OTC contacts are bilateral, and each party could face credit risk regarding its counterparty. Moreover the lack of transparency and weaker liquidity the flexibility of derivative contract design can worsen the situation. OTC derivative market deals in forward contract, foreign exchange swaps and option. In forward OTC market, the terms of the contract are agreed upon the trade date for execution at a future date decided between the parties to the contract, It provide quotes for booking a forward contract for any maturity. Liquidity is high for maturity less than one year and beyond that liquidity is less, while it is possible to book forward contact at any maturity. The settlement can be on gross basis or net basis. Foreign currency swap is an instrument used to hedge risk arising out of the exposure to a currency by the exchange of liability.

(D) Exchange Traded Derivative

Such contracts are standardized derivative contracts available on recognized stock exchanges permitted to deal in currency derivatives by SEBI and by RBI. It includes option, future and other contracts that are listed and traded on exchange. Person who have payment obligation in foreign currency in future can buy a currency pair future that will lock in the price today, depreciation in Rupee will not affect.

CHAPTER EIGHTEEN

Risk & Return

All investment involves uncertainty and are risk prone. Investment is made in the present time, with an expectation to earn in the future. Risk in investment is the probability that the expected return may diminish in some manner or other. Risks in investment means actual return differ from expected return. All securities tend to have some systematic as well as unsystematic risk. Hence risk are of two types.

A. Systematic Risk
B. Un systematic Risk

(A) Systematic Risk is risk for the market as a whole, it is attributable to macro factors and effecting all securities. It reflect the impact of political, economic & financial factors.

(B) Un systematic Risk is the risk unique to a specific security, and associated with liquidity risk, business risk, management risk.

Both the systematic and unsystematic risk are additive to derive total risk.

Total Risk = Systematic Risk +Un systematic Risk.

DIFFERENT TYPES OF RISK.

1) Market Risk – The volatility in security returns, from the fluctuation in the market is market risk. It includes war, tax, recessions & etc. And may be categorize under systematic risk.

2) Interest Rate Risk – Change in security returns rate from change in interest rates is interest rate risk. Security price moves inversely, as interest rate change Bond price moves in opposite direction.

3) Inflation Risk Or Purchasing Power Risk – Due to inflation risk the inflow the inflow from an investment may be less when they have been adjusted for inflation. Interest rates rise as inflation increase, as lender demand additional inflation premium to adjust for the loss of purchasing power.

4) Default Risk – It is also known as credit risk that results from changes in the financial integrity of the investment, if borrower could default to repay principal or interest on the due dates. The failure by a borrower to honor to pay interest or principal or both creates default risk.

5) Liquidity Risk – Absence of liquidity in an investment is a risk. If investor may not be able to sell investment when desired, its liquidity risk. Equity market are not exposed to liquidity risk. But fixed return investments are exposed to risk. If Fixed Deposit are broken before maturity some penalty may be imposed and so on.

6) Re Investment Risk – Such risk are loss from re investing principal or interest or both. Risk will affect if interest rate fall and on the other hand receivable interest will be not be same with the same invested principal.

7) Business Risk - Doing business itself is risky, business effected by many internal and external forces and that

remain threat to firm and its management team. Macro economic factors like political, technology, environmental, legal, economic are beyond the control of management. Risk at firm level may inefficient management, reputation, corporate culture etc.

8) Management Risk – If management do any sort of mistake can harm those who invested in their firms. Risk may be due to ethical, financial or any other sort of wrong decision. Which ultimately affect the efficiency, quality of the end product. Such risk associated with managing an investment is management risk.

MEASUREMENT OF RISK

Risk is the uncertainty of a future outcome. Return from investment for future period is expected return. Return over past period is realized return. Realized return may be the basis while investing. Few methods of investing are below

A. Volatility
B. Standard Deviation
C. Beta

A. **Volatility** – The range of movement from the expected level of return. The more a stock goes up and down in price, more volatile the stock is. Due to swing in price, there is uncertainty of an eventual outcome. More volatile more risk is there.
B. **Standard Deviation** – Deviation meant, how much individual data deviate from the MEAN. In investment standard deviation measures the volatility associated with investment relative to its rate of return.
C. **Beta** – It measures the individual security volatility, fluctuation in price relative to a benchmark, the market

portfolio of all stocks. In other words Beta is the risk of an individual stock relative to the Stock Market portfolio of all stocks.

RETURN

Investment is made in the present time and inflows come in future. Measuring return in investment simply compare the capitalce outflow with the inflow. Return may be positive or negative, if returns are positive then gain is there and vice versa. Return from investment may even appreciate or depreciate and value may not be paid out or got deducted from anywhere like gold price or piece of land.

FACTORS OF RISK

a. Nature of instrument, either it is debt or equity.
b. Equity shares are considered more risky investment.
c. The ability of borrower to repay interest in due date as well as return back capital.
d. Time period, the longer the maturity period, less the risk is.

a. Never borrow for investing purpose.

DETERMINANTS OF RETURN EXPECTED BY INVESTOR.

a. Risk associated with the unique investment.
b. Time preference risk free rate.
c. Expected rate of inflation.

All three determinants are additive.

Return = Risk free rate + Inflation Premium + Risk Premium.

Risk Return Relationship

Risk and Return are directly variables i.e. an investment with higher risk produce higher return. In simple words, investors who expect higher return, willing to take higher risk, whereas investors who do not want to take risk get low return. Return is reward to the investors for bearing risk in an investment. The tent of investment is that there is a tradeoff between risk and return. Growth assets give higher return and have a higher risk, Income assts show a lower return with lower risk. Investor selects the risk return combination that suits their requirement.

In investment risk is the chance that an investment actual return will be different than expected, risk is possibility of losing some or all original investment. Riskier is the assets higher will be the risk premium. The risk free return is taken as the Government borrowing rate and risk premium is the difference between the return of risky asset and the risk free rate of return.

Investor selects investments that are consistent with their risk preference. The risk return tradeoff means higher risk may have the possibility of higher return but there is no guarantee. Risk means higher potential returns and otherwise higher potential loss. Risk tolerance differs from person to person while determining risk level, it depends on goals, income and personal situation among other factors.

Portfolio & Security Returns

A portfolio is a combination of various securities instrument. The principle in constructing a portfolio is to enhance the benefits of diversification. If investments are made in a particular type of instrument, it will be impacted by the risk factors it is exposed to. While constructing portfolio one must check all instrument are not exposed to the same risk factor. Any point of time, one instrument may be earning a higher return, while other may not. A short term debt instrument performs well but equity investment would do well in another, where positive return for investing in equity may have a negative return for debt. Investing across different instrument provides the benefits of diversifying risk, they cancel out risks of one another to some extent called the diversification benefits.

Portfolio Diversification and Risk

In statistic correlation is relationship whether casual or otherwise between two random variables, if they change together at a constant rate. Whereas in investment correlation provides information whether the asset class returns are moving in same direction and what is the extent to which they move together. The extent to which risk reduced by combining two assets depends upon the correlation between various assets. If return from equity and debt, going up and down together, there is no benefit of combining these two. If they move in opposite direction, an investor can achieve a risk level of zero by combining the two assets class. But in reality to achieve zero risk portfolio is not sounding good , no one invest to get zero return for any investment. Investor can reduce risk by bringing in assets class that do not move in the same direction. Correlation range in between +1 to -1. As long as correlation between two assets class is less than one, some risk reduction is possible by combining them in a portfolio. Diversification does not eliminates risk or guarantee return, it reduces the volatility in the returns of a portfolio. While constructing and managing an investment portfolio, the focus is always on generating a better risk adjusted return. The gain in risk reduction from portfolio diversification depends inversely upon the extent to which the returns on the securities in a portfolio are positively correlated. Ideally the security should display negative correlation.

Risk & Return of Portfolio

Expected return from portfolio is equal to the weighted average of the expected returns from the individual securities.

Rp = Wa (Ra) + Wb (Rb)

Where

Rp = Expected return from a portfolio of two instruments

Wa = Proportion of funds invested in instrument A

Wb = Proportion of fund invested in instrument B

Ra = Expected return of instrument A

Rb = Expected return of instrument B

Wa + Wb =1

CHAPTER NINETEEN

Tax Implication

TAXES are of two types

Direct tax – As per section 14, of The income tax Act, income of a person is computed under the following five heads

I. Salaries
II. Income from house property
III. Profits and gains of business or profession

I. Capital gain
II. Income from other sources.

Since we are concerned with the tax implication on gain and profits from sell or buy of shares it comes under the head capital gains.

Under section 45(1), any profit or gain arising from the transfer of a capital asset is chargeable to tax under the head "capital gain" in the previous year in which the transfer took place.

Capital Assets mean property of any kind held by an assesse whether or not connected with his business or profession. There are two types of capital assets Long term and Short term assets. A short term capital assets mean capital asset held by an assesse for not more than 36 months, immediately prior to its date of transfer. However in the following cases an asset held for not more than 12 month is treated as short term capital assets.

(i) Equity or preference shares in a company (whether shares are quoted or not)

(ii) Securities (like debentures, Govt. securities) listed in a recognized stock exchange in India.

(iii) Units of UTI (whether quoted or not)

(iv) Units of mutual fund specified under section 10(23D) whether quoted or not.

Assets other than short term assets are regarded as Long term assets.

TAX LAIBILITY ON SHARES

Bonus share- The cost of acquisition of any additional financial asset as bonus shares or security or otherwise which is received without any payment by the assesse on the basis of his holding any financial assets shall be taken to NIL.

Right Share – There was no specific provision dealing with determination of the cost of financial instrument such as right shares, however the cost of the right shares is equal to the cost incurred by him for purchasing the right entitlement plus the price paid by him to the company for acquiring the right shares.

Conversion of debenture into shares – Any transfer by way of conversion of debentures, of a company into shares or debentures of that company is not regarded as a transfer giving rise to any capital gains. On sale of share or debentures received on such conversion the capital gain shall be computed by taking the cost of acquisition as that part of the cost of debentures, which has been appropriated toward the share or debentures.

Transfer of stock option or sweat equity

When share is offered to employee by the employer, the difference between the market value of shares and the cost at which it is offered to the employee is taxable as perquisites.

However under section 54EA, 54EB exemption is available.

In case of long term Capital gain arising out of shares, the tax rate is 10% excluding any cess or surcharge, if the gain amount is above one lakh. No indexation facility is available to seller. Securities other than ones mentioned in Section 112A are also subject to taxation.

Securities Transaction Tax

It is levied on each purchase or sale of every security that is listed in stock market. This includes securities such as shares, equity mutual funds and derivatives. The STT rate for equity transaction i.e. for both buying and selling is 0.1% of the total value. The STT is zero for purchase and 0.25% of the turnover value while selling the security.

Dividend Distribution Tax

It is levied on companies declaring dividend to their shareholder, however Govt. abolish DTT, and now companies can share all the distributable profit with shareholders. However the recipient of the dividend is likely to pay tax as per the applicable rates.

Thanks for reading.

To learn more explore the additional resource

www.nseindia.com

www.bseindia.com

www.nsdl.co.in

www.nism.ac.in

visit the NCFM window at www.nseindia.com

www.ingramcontent.com/pod-product-compliance
Ingram Content Group UK Ltd.
Pitfield, Milton Keynes, MK11 3LW, UK
UKHW021935190726
13853UKWH00004B/1465

9 798888 056844